# Praise for

When we look at the educati ⸻ quickly understand the importance that safe and supportive learning environments play, and why they should be at the forefront of all educator's minds. Challenges arise, however, when we start to look to the application of best practices and strategies to help support students and staff in our schools by establishing and sustaining these positive spaces. In *Rising Above*, JC Pohl is able to take what can often times be a daunting experience and provide real life, replicable solutions to help educators understand how to shift from theory to practice in understanding and meeting the needs of students and staff in our schools.

–Adam Lustig, Director, Leadership Services,
Education & Training, National
School Boards Association

As long as there are schools there will be conflict. But it doesn't have to be the knock-down-drag-out kind. By writing this book as a fable about a fictitious school counselor, Pohl helps educators learn how to defuse typical school conflicts by showing us the way this counselor approaches conflict, speaks to those involved, and intentionally builds relationships–the true antidote to all conflicts.

–Jenn David-Lang, THE MAIN IDEA,
Learn & Lead: Masterminds for School Leaders

The salvation of public education is rooted in all stakeholders realizing we are on the same team. JC Pohl provides an insightful incorporation of key culture tenets, based on today's realities, in a refreshing, hopeful, urgently needed playbook.

–Mary Jane Hetrick, PhD, School Board President,
Dripping Springs ISD, Texas

As an education leader, I have learned that maintaining a safe and student-centered environment can be accomplished simply by calming school conflict. JC Pohl has delivered a book that not only helps to give school leaders strategies to minimize conflict but also provides a tool that can be used to engage this issue with my staff and campus community. JC's story-driven approach is refreshing, applicable, and uniquely different from most school culture books I have read.

–Dr. Pete M. Getz, Ed.D., Principal,
Valencia High School, California

# RISING ABOVE

# RISING ABOVE

## A Story of Positive School Conflict Resolution

JC Pohl
*with*
Ryan McKernan

JB JOSSEY-BASS™
A Wiley Brand

JCP: This book is dedicated to my mother, Jean Pohl. I don't think I have ever truly been in conflict with her, but for my entire life she has taught me to see the world with clear eyes and a full heart. I love you, Mom!

RM: This work is dedicated to my fiancée, Ali. Thank you for all your love, and for reminding me to take a break every now and then.

# ALSO FROM JC POHL, LMFT

*Building School Culture from the Inside Out*
*Building Resilient Students from the Inside Out*
*Building Campus Relationships from the Inside Out*
*TEEN TRUTH: Why Youth Have Something to Hide*
*RISING UP: Coaching Program – Curriculum Handbook*

The TEEN TRUTH Film Series

# CONTENTS

# PREFACE

In the briefest terms possible, conflict is best handled when broken down into two steps: connect and collaborate. Through these two steps, we can collectively rise above the challenges we face.

I know it isn't often that an author writes his own Preface. Usually this spot in the book is reserved for some kind of famous, influential voice that lends credibility and support to the project, but I did not obtain this information from a pool of famous people. After years on the road, building school culture through assemblies and workshops with TEEN TRUTH, I learned these lessons from school leaders like you.

In meeting so many of you, I realized that if I picked out a few of the best practices that I'd seen work *really* well at each school, put it together in a book, and offered it to educators as a resource, then teachers would be able to learn, adopt, and practice those strategies they believed would help their school the most.

This book seeks to do that. In that way, it's a little different. I don't want to tell you what to do, because the ins and outs of your school are best known to you. Instead, I decided to tell a story that I had seen happen personally. This story is of a composite character named Monica who teaches at Serenity Springs High School. Monica represents all the best teachers, counselors, and administrators that I've met throughout my years who have figured out ways to impart a tremendous, positive impact in their schools.

For this book, I reached out to a handful of people who succeeded regularly, specifically in addressing conflict. Each of them possesses vast experience and knowledge on the subjects addressed in this book, so I will make sure to point you to each of them as a reference. If you find value in this book, then you will find value in their work.

I've visited a lot of schools. Since 2006 I have been traveling across the country, listening to students and teachers voice their truth as they build school culture across North America. My mission was (and is) to cultivate a positive school climate in those communities. I have worked in every type of school community that you can imagine and with every type of school leader you can think of. At the time of writing this book, I personally have walked onto 1,243 campuses. Through TEEN TRUTH we have reached 11,285,800 students. In that time I have learned one thing with absolute clarity:

You, the people who work at those schools, are amazing. The work you do is amazing. The people you serve are amazing. The catch is that school conflict arises naturally and can sometimes feel like it's ruining your progress. At first glance, it might appear that conflict deflates our hearts and detracts from our mission, but that only occurs if we choose to see it as a fight. A battle. A war with blood and tears. That's certainly how I used to perceive conflict.

But in my travels, I began to see that there were people who approached conflict differently. I met people who somehow managed to negotiate what I thought was guaranteed to be a knock-down-drag-out fight without having things escalate, and with *both* parties walking away better off than before.

Through several interviews with those experts, I slowly came to understand how they manage to do this. It's something anyone can learn, and everyone will benefit from. To help, I have added elements from these interviews as part of Monica's journal, as well as included all of the best points at the very end of this book.

This book was written to show you what that looks like through a story. One thing I've certainly learned from teachers is that examples go a long way.

With that in mind, I hope this story inspires and supports your own efforts to find positive resolution in your own conflicts. While the characters and stories in this book are fictional, they are based in reality. Many of you will recognize the archetypes portrayed in this book: a parent who is really concerned about how a school does things; a student who simply does not connect; a teacher who has been doing this job so long they have forgotten why, and if they could just find that spark again . . .

Through our protagonist's viewpoint, I want to offer you realistic examples that you can use immediately to start defusing conflict and improving campus culture. To do so, I interviewed the best experts I know in all aspects of the education field. They charted out a map that you can use in every aspect of your job (and your life). I hope you will find your time at Serenity Springs High School valuable and that when you do face that school conflict coming at you from all different directions that you will know exactly how to start *rising above.*

# FEATURED EXPERTS

Emil Harker
Licensed Marriage and Family Therapist

Dr. Pete Getz
Valencia High School Principal

Dr. Stephanie Eberts
Assistant Professor of Professional Practice at Louisiana
State University

Dr. Mary Jane Hetrick
School Board President for Dripping Springs Independent School District

Adam Lustig
Director for Leadership Services and Training for the
National School Boards Association

Tamara Gives
Granite Bay High School Activities Director

# CONFLICT

# CHAPTER ONE

# OMELETS AND ARGUMENTS

If you want to make an omelet, you've got to break some eggs, but that doesn't mean you need to make a mess of things. You can crack the shells over the pan instead of on your counter. With a little practice, you'll manage to keep the contents of the egg completely in the pan. Whisking doesn't need to be a violent action in order to be effective. You can stir decisively without spilling. The vegetables you chop can be kept in an orderly fashion on the cutting board, and gently corralled into the pan. Ultimately, saving yourself from having to clean up egg residue from your counter requires much less effort than it does to recklessly smash, scrape, hack, and blend an omelet together.

Monica practiced that mindfulness as she stood in front of her stove. She had learned the lesson after enduring countless chaotic preparations followed by many hours cleaning up after several needlessly messy omelets.

That lesson, like the many she had realized over her past few years of leading an examined life, offered a safe haven of calm and clarity in a daily moment that had once been a chore.

Monica's husband, Mike, prepared the other components of breakfast nearby. He took his time, arranging a small parfait for both of them. The two of them had learned to move harmoniously in their small kitchen, and their little cooking dance was one of the games that Monica enjoyed most. The shared activity helped them to start off their day on the same wavelength.

They had not always enjoyed such a harmonious existence together. They had very nearly ended their marriage just five years ago. Back then, they consistently fell into heated arguments, and fought about seemingly trivial issues. Despite loving each other sincerely, they just couldn't get along. Worse still, the fights never seemed to actually resolve or improve anything.

Their relationship had been saved one night after a particularly rough disagreement when they realized they had a choice to make: learn how to work as a team together, or split up.

They both agreed that night to go all in on trying to make things work. What followed next was a long but rewarding journey. They started with marriage counseling and worked together to develop all their communication skills. Through those communications skills, they learned that the main source of their problem was in the way they handled conflict.

Their default model went straight to criticism, and as a result each of them had been constantly on the defensive. Realizing this, they learned a new but still very simple model from which they first found connection and then collaboration.

Together, they figured out why neither of them had developed a more functional model of conflict resolution. Mike had grown up in a conflict-avoidant home, and as a result, had trouble engaging in conflict until he had already reached a defensive emotional state. Over time, Monica understood that Mike was conflict avoidant not out of apathy, but out of a sincere love and desire for harmony. His defensive reaction wasn't because he was frail, but because he was truly trying his best and demanded a lot of himself.

In turn, Mike discovered that conflict was a big part of growth, and a cornerstone for a healthy relationship. Mike ultimately learned that Monica's inclination to address issues directly and immediately came from the same place of love. Monica wasn't nagging, Mike realized, she was advocating for the relationship to be as wonderful as they both knew it could be. She didn't want problems to fester and create a divide between them. She truly wanted harmony just as much as he did.

Back then, she didn't know how to address conflict in a collaborative way. A combination of media and her upbringing had conditioned her to believe that life was a zero-sum game, and that a scarcity-oriented, competition-driven mindset was the only way for her needs to be met.

She realized she needed a new approach.

She began to try to look at conflict not in terms of competition and scarcity, but in terms of cooperation and abundance. In time, she learned that this point of view tended to deliver better results for both the other person *and* her.

Conflict, she realized, is best handled when broken down into two steps: connection and collaboration.

That was the beginning of the work. Over the years, the two of them got pretty darn good at establishing connection first and collaboration second.

The changes were small at first, but in time, the minutia aggregated into noticeable differences in their relationship. Gratitude grew. They began going on dates again. Mike began taking initiative in planning events. Conflicts resolved more easily. Then, one day Monica woke up and looked at Mike lying next to her. His head had slid off his pillow in the night, and he was drooling on the bed. As strange as it might sound, in that moment she realized she had fallen in love with him once again. They had put in the work and had found genuine happiness in each other.

They weren't perfect, of course. The two of them still stumbled, from time to time, but communication can be developed just like any other skill. The relationship blossomed.

Today was a warm, pleasant day. Outside, birds chirped over the sound of the city coming alive. Clouds passed across the sky, lazily. As Monica and Mike ate their omelet and parfait breakfast, Monica noticed a challenging feeling in the pit of her stomach. The feeling weighed heavily and emanated a foreboding nausea. She took a moment to go into the sensation, examining it and allowing herself to familiarize herself with what her body was telling her.

"I'm kind of anxious about starting today," Monica told her husband.

"Yeah?" Mike replied, providing space for her to finish her thought.

Monica had diligently researched and prepared for her new position as counselor at Serenity Springs High School, but she still felt anxious. The school had a lot of problems. Despite the fact that the staff was experienced and capable, there were a lot of issues that needed to be resolved. Student engagement was low by any reasonable metric, grades were subpar, attendance was poor, and disciplinary action was slightly higher than average. None of these problems were particularly overwhelming in and of themselves, but the aggregate of all of them, Monica knew, was a strong indication that there were underlying school culture issues that needed to be addressed.

But for now, in this moment, Monica was sitting in her kitchen, eating breakfast with Mike. The stress of the day had not yet arrived, and by displacing herself away from the present moment, she was accomplishing nothing except for generating needless anxiety.

"It'll be alright," Monica concluded. "I just needed to come back to the present."

Mike nodded.

Monica considered asking Mike to pick up the milk, but realized he too was under a lot of stress. Rather than thoughtlessly add a task to his day, she decided to open up the discussion with her partner so they could collaborate and decide together.

"So . . . who's picking up milk today?" Monica asked.

"I'm headed to the north office, so my route is a ways away from milk," Mike suggested.

"That's true," Monica conceded, "but I've got an earlier start and a later end for my day, so from a total time invested point of view, logistics kind of break even."

"Truth," Mike said, "and honestly, I'm not bothered by the extra drive because that history podcast I've been listening to is getting *good.*"

"That's cool. Will you fill me in on it at dinner tonight?" Monica asked.

"Abso-tively posi-lutely," Mike answered.

A chuckle escaped Monica. Mike was an unapologetic dork, and for some reason the weird little things he did always got her to laugh.

"Alright, alright," Monica said, "I know I'm stressed about starting, but I know you're training a whole bunch of new people and that's stressful too, so . . . mental and emotional strain is probably pretty even?"

"Yup. So that means . . . there's only one fair way to settle this," Mike suggested, balling his right hand up on top of his left hand. He loved leaving such matters to chance and didn't even try to conceal his excitement.

"Rock, paper, scissors, shoot!"

The tasks and logistics were even. The emotional strain was even. Chance is fair, and Mike was going to pick up the milk today. Monica scooped up her lifeline—a journal that she had used to collect notes from all of her best advisors—and began the next part of her day.

# CHAPTER TWO

# TROUBLE IN SERENITY

The halls of Serenity Springs High School were still quiet when Monica arrived at the school. The building was well kept, with the school colors of navy blue and orange patterned occasionally on the predominately white tile floors. The bottom two-thirds of the painted brick walls held that same, comforting blue, interrupted at the perfect height by a decisive orange line two bricks thick, running all the way down the hall. Above that, both colors gave way to a smooth, eggshell white, which converged perfectly with the perforated ceiling tiles, which Monica noted were present in virtually every school in America.

Monica's coffee had cooled off just enough for her to enjoy it comfortably as she took a lap around the school.

She took smooth, steady breaths in between sips, savoring the hazelnut notes and pleasant warmth in her mouth.

A handful of teachers who had arrived early took care of those hidden tasks that kept the school running. Monica smiled and greeted each teacher with a sunny "Good morning." She took care to feel authentic gratitude toward each of them with every greeting.

Monica knew that the teachers were the undisputed lynch-pin to every school. She admired their efforts and recognized that her role as a counselor could only ever be effective if she held their trust. She also knew that such trust would only be given once the teachers knew she sincerely had their best interests in mind.

Monica's office was two doors down from the office of Principal Hannah Shore. Principal Shore's door was open, and Monica knocked gently on the edge of the door and peeked in to see if it was a good time to check in.

Although she was on the phone, Principal Shore smiled and waved Monica into the room. Monica sat down in a comfort-able chair on the guest's side of the principal's desk.

The desk itself was tidy, with two stacks of documents, one on either side of Principal Shore's half of the desk. Shore's computer was set just off to the left side and rotated diag-onally, so that it would not obstruct any conversation with anyone sitting across from her. By the principal's left hand sat a large white mug with bold blue text that appeared to be hand-painted onto it. The text read:

*Where there is unity, there is always victory.*

"I understand," Shore was saying in a tone that begged for de-escalation, "of course, yes. Thank you for bringing it to my attention, I'll look into it straight away . . . of course, yes . . . I–yes . . ."

That tone carried on for a few more minutes before Principal Shore finally untangled herself from the audible tirade on the other side enough to end the call. Monica pieced together the fact that the call was from a parent who was very upset about the new bus schedule, specifically, the fact that the bus dropped the kids off at their home last.

"Hoo! Some people get upset so easily!" Principal Shore confided.

"Yeah, that sounded intense. Is it a talk-about-it thing, or a leave-it-be thing?" Monica asked.

"Oh, just a pick-your-battles kind of thing," Shore answered, picking up on Monica's cadence. "You know how some parents can be! They all want what's best for their kids, but some of them don't understand how things work. But enough about that! How are you feeling about your first day?"

Monica made a casual note of Shore's statement in her mind. That parent had been loud enough in her complaints that Monica could hear her from where she sat. Certainly Principal Shore's patience and understanding were admirable, but Monica wondered for a moment if Principal Shore got berated like that often. She realized that Shore's tone even seemed to anticipate a complaint from Monica herself.

"I was a little nervous this morning but now that I'm here, I feel great! I've got what I need to get started. I'm excited to help, and happy to be a part of this team," Monica answered, wanting to send the signal right away that the two of them were indeed on the same team, and that she wasn't about to throw undue grief or burden on anyone.

"Oh, well that's good to hear!" Principal Shore seemed relieved.

"Absolutely. I just wanted to stop by and double-check to see how you're doing. I'm here to support everyone, and that includes you. Running a school is a really challenging thing to do," Monica said.

"It is! Education is a tough gig," admitted Principal Shore, "but we can handle it if we work together."

"Speaking of which, did you make that mug?" Monica asked. "The calligraphy is amazing."

"I did! It's sort of a hobby of mine. I used to have horrible handwriting so—"

The phone rang, interrupting the conversation.

". . . to be continued," Principal Shore said.

"Can't wait to hear and see more, Principal Shore." Monica smiled as she got up.

"Oh, you can call me Hannah. We're teammates, right?"

"Right."

On her way out she overheard Principal Shore greeting the caller warmly, despite the attitude she had dealt with from the previous caller just a few moments ago. But on the other end it sounded like another complaint being launched against her. Monica couldn't help but detect a tone of defeat in Principal Shore's voice. It reminded her of something she had learned from the principal at her last school, Dr. Pete Getz. As Monica took care of her morning tasks, she recalled the lesson she had written down in her journal.

## Monica's Journal

## Dr. Pete Getz on Feeling Overwhelmed

- Connect to the elements of education that got you to where you are.
  - You are finally in the place you wanted to be.
- Practice self-care and a healthy balance between work and personal life.
  - Find things in your life that you enjoy and go do them!

# CHAPTER THREE

# THE OUTBURST

Betty's cheeks were pink with anger, and she was trying to keep herself calm by taking slow, steady breaths. Unfortunately her student, Tony, was not letting up. He had been acting out all day, and the moment Betty had tried to correct his behavior, he had gotten argumentative and hostile.

"It's all bullshit anyway," Tony insisted "after you graduate, they just stick you in a desk and work you 'til you're dead. This is a waste of time."

"No it's not," Betty insisted. "You're just being pessimistic."

"Yes, Ms. Betty, I am indeed being pessimistic. What an astute observation! I do, in fact, feel highly pessimistic about this entire system, and where it's headed."

"What does any of that have to do with learning calculus?" Betty said.

She couldn't believe this kid, and she was even more frustrated that she had to keep her kid gloves on in her responses. She wanted to show him the truth as she understood it, that the world was full of people who were trying to make things better and that, on the whole, they did pretty well. She wanted to point out that he was making these complaints with a full stomach, in an air-conditioned environment, to somebody who actively wanted him to succeed, but it was hard to get a word in edgewise when everything had to go through the be-a-positive-adult-role-model filter.

Tony was getting increasingly upset as he continued down his own rabbit hole. "What does that have to do with calculus? Everything! All of it is connected! Each part of the system is *part* of the system, and so it all acts within that system. The system itself is broken, and so each part reflects the inherent brokenness of the entire shitty-ass system."

"Watch your language," Betty interjected, "and Tony, regardless of your outlooks, I have a class to teach, and right now you're disrupting it."

"So what? What is a disruption anyway? Breaking away from the order of things? Isn't that good? When the order of things pumps out depressed and anxious kids that hit record suicide rates yearly?" Tony's voice was rising. "I think the main problem here is that we don't have *enough* disruptions! So, yeah! I'm a disruption!"

"Tony, you are on thin ice. I am sick and tired of these outbursts!"

Tony stood up and put his hands in the air. "All hail the outburst! Behold the disruption! The dissenter! The one who sees through the bullshit!"

Betty was at a loss for words. She had tried everything she could think of. She had tried negotiating, being authoritative, and directly calling Tony out on his behavior. Nothing worked.

"Tony! If you're going to insist on interrupting my lessons with your ranting–"

"Oh, that wasn't a rant!" Tony was yelling now. "You want to hear a rant? Kids shouldn't be sitting down for six hours a day! Kids shouldn't be forced to wake up at six in the morning! People shouldn't have to be expected to act like machines! You're trying to do something that literally goes against every natural impulse all of us have, and I have yet to see any benefit to this stupid way of life! The only reason you're upset with me is because you can't think for yourself! You're a robot! You're just another brainless cog!"

Tony had crossed a line. Even as he said it, he knew he was in the wrong, regardless of the points he was trying to make, and the fact that Betty could see some truth to them, he was so far out of line that she could not let it stand.

"Out," Betty pointed decisively to the door.

"I didn't mean–"

"Out!" Betty exclaimed. "I am done with you for today! Get out of my classroom!"

Tony snatched his backpack up angrily and stomped up the aisle between his peers' desks. The class watched in shock as he threw the door open, stopped, turned around, and announced, "Yes, of course! I will follow your orders! I will not think for myself! I am your slave!" before marching away down the hall.

Betty somehow managed to resist firing back with any of the half dozen quips that came to her mind. She was furious now. Part of her was angry at the audacity of this kid, to speak to anyone that way. Another part of her was angry that she had to work so hard to restrain herself and couldn't defend herself the way she wanted to. If anyone ever spoke to her that way outside of school, she would *never* have put up with it. She would have absolutely ripped into anyone else who spoke to her that way. After all, she was a Jersey girl growing up and had spent enough time at baseball games with her brothers to know how to really lay into someone, but because he was a student, and because she was a teacher, she knew she had to find a way to be the adult in the situation. But she didn't want to be the adult. She wanted to be herself. It was all so tiring, striving to act as a role model for her students day after day, especially when she knew in her heart that at least part of her agreed with some of his views. Betty supposed that navigating all such feelings was the point of being the adult in the room. She gave herself a little grace and remembered that her feelings were always justified; the important part was how she handled them.

She took in a very deep breath through her nose. *Don't let him get in your head. You're a professional,* she thought to herself, *and one bad apple isn't going to ruin your day. These kids want to learn. Do not let him steal the magic from the other students. Ha . . . really, this is nothing compared to what you've handled before. You've been through worse. You can handle this.*

"Sorry for the disruption, class. Thank you for being patient. Now . . . we were learning about derivatives," Betty calmly continued. "We're looking at this roller coaster, we're headed up, we're headed down, so we can't use a slope to measure the roller coaster's movement because the movement is always changing. With me so far? Good. Okay, so the power of derivatives . . . is how to calculate . . . the rate of change *at any given point.* That's a pretty powerful thing to know, right?"

The class picked up again, and slowly shifted back into its usual order, but the exchange didn't sit well with Betty.

The personal insult was enough to leave her fired up, but she was secure in herself. She was perfectly confident about who she was, but that boy was a problem. His outbursts were, she was sure, more than just typical teenage rebellion. Typical teenage rebellion was something she could relate to. She had gone through her own rebel phase at that age, and it had served her very well. The lessons she learned during that time had helped her to cultivate a strong sense of resiliency and self-efficacy. Her rebellion was more about fun and defying authority with your friends by staying out too late and listening to punk rock. But this was different. She didn't like playing the part of the authoritarian, and she wasn't even particularly strict, but for some reason Tony lashed out at her as if her classroom was some sort of bootcamp.

She didn't want to deal with this. She *couldn't* deal with this, not in a class as advanced as this one. The calculus curriculum was hard enough without any interruptions, but if Tony's behavior continued, these kids certainly wouldn't hit their goals. It saddened her to think of how different he was this year. Last year he'd breezed through her precalculus class. This year he was already causing her to dread her third hour.

She realized this was not something to be taken on alone. *That new counselor did say she was settled in and happy to help us with anything,* Betty recalled, *so let's test that hypothesis.*

# CHAPTER FOUR

# ONLINE BUT DISCONNECTED

Sandra was about to delete her post, but then she saw that it had 40 likes. That was twice as many as she usually got. It read:

> So . . . are we just gonna snatch boys up behind each other's backs? what happened 2 sisters? fake people r fake and rhyme with jambalaya

Sandra had felt bad when she'd originally posted it. She had become jealous and angry when she heard that Maya and Norbert had been spotted hanging out together after school. Sandra had told Maya that she was interested in Norbert just a week ago, and now Sandra felt betrayed.

Sandra made the post partially to let off some steam, but also to see how her followers reacted. It seemed like they were in agreement with her, just by the number of likes the post had gotten. Nobody had posted a response yet, but Sandra took their likes to mean that they agreed with her, and that Maya was being sneaky and was in the wrong. She decided to take another stab at the sneaky snake. Sandra leaned against her locker and tried to think of what to post next.

```
new game: if ur a snake have ur name
rhymes with papaya
```

*Is that mean?* Sandra wondered, *No, it's no big deal. It's just funny. Besides, that's what she gets for going behind my back. Should I post it?*

She had a few minutes to think. The school day was over, and her aunt was picking her up today. Her aunt was usually a little bit late, so Sandra had a little time to catch up on social media and hang out around the school. She began to take her familiar lap down to the gymnasium. Sometimes she liked to sit and watch the other kids play basketball. Sandra wasn't the sort to want to be on the court. She felt much more comfortable watching, which is how she had found herself spending time at most games. She didn't even really care too much for sports, she just wanted to be around people, even if it was just as an anonymous member of the crowd.

The girls' basketball team had just started practicing. Sandra made her way to the very top of the bleachers, in her favorite corner where nobody ever looked up. She was happy there, alone with her thoughts but with people to watch. She was jealous of the stories her older sister told her, about hanging out in busy malls, eating buttery pretzels and chatting the afternoon away. It was strange for her, to feel nostalgia for something she had never experienced but still knew she was missing.

She looked down at her phone, and at the message she had typed out. Forty likes. Forty people. Maybe she wasn't isolated because the mall was empty. Maybe she just hadn't taken enough initiative. Forty people had noticed her. Her! She was the one that was always nearby but never got any attention. Did things have to be that way? This was at least one way of finding out.

She sent the post.

Instantly, she felt a drop in her stomach like she had almost lost control on her bike. It was a nauseous feeling deep down inside that made her face twist down into a frown. She really did not like the feeling. She was glad she was up, away from other people, because it felt like there was a slime monster inside of her that had managed to take over. All at once, she felt embarrassed and gross.

"Okay, no more," she said out loud to herself.

But as Sandra was about to put her phone away, she noticed she'd already gotten a like on her new post.

Maybe she wasn't the only one who had been backstabbed by Maya. Could it be that she was just that way, and everybody already knew it, and Sandra was the first to say anything about it? Maybe the bad feeling she had felt was only because she wasn't used to standing up for herself.

Maybe things really were black and white. Maybe this sting she felt wasn't exactly rooted in reality, and part of growing up was setting those feelings aside to do what needed to be done. Even though she didn't know the whole situation, it was at least possible that she was right. All she had to go on was hearsay, but wasn't that the way most information was passed along?

There could be a number of explanations, including that Maya was being a bad friend. And even though Sandra hadn't actually spoken to Norbert yet, she had definitely told Maya about her crush on him and had gone on and on about how impressed she was with him for winning the regional spelling bee.

Or maybe she was being too hard on Maya. Maybe all of this was just silly, and she should just drop it and go talk to her friend. Maybe she should take down her most recent post. Posting it must have made her feel bad for a reason, right? Isn't that what her big sister had said? "It isn't as complicated as all those philosophers make it out to be. Everyone knows what's wrong, because the wrong thing feels wrong."

*It does feel wrong. Should I delete that post, then? Yes, that's definitely the right thing to do,* Sandra thought to herself as she turned back down to her phone, *I should delete all of that negativity and go talk to Maya. She's been my friend since fifth grade, and I should at least hear her side of the story. Yes, that's the best choice. That's what I'm going to do.*

But just as she was about to press the delete button, another "like" popped up.

Then another.

And another.

# CHAPTER FIVE

# RED VS. BLUE

Monica sat in the teacher's lounge, enjoying her lunch with a handful of teachers. They were a thoughtful and fun crew with big ideas and strong opinions. Monica spent most of her time on that first day listening to them, asking about their interests, and just having fun in the present moment with them.

The lounge was not glamorous, but it was big enough. There was a coffee maker which was used relentlessly throughout the day, a pair of refrigerators which were already full, and just enough seating for everyone to enjoy a comfortable lunch break. The chat eventually turned to politics, and as is often the case, the discussion focused around the most controversial issue.

Currently, two local political opponents had captured almost everyone's attention. On one side of the aisle, you had Captain James Dirk, and on the other, Dr. Kathryn Spocard.

"I really just think Dirk's got it all figured out," Frank insisted. "He leads by his gut! He's got his own values and he sticks to 'em. If something is right, he just does it, even if it does go against some silly rule, who cares?"

"Who cares?" Cara shot back. "The laws exist for a reason! For goodness sakes Frank, our leaders need to lead by logic and resolve! We need a real adult in office, not some cowboy."

"What's wrong with cowboys? Don't cowboys get things done? Spocard has no heart! You look at her and there's no emotion! Heck, she prides herself on being emotionless. We might as well have a computer running things," Frank said.

"If only," Cara said before turning back to her applesauce.

"How about you?" Frank said, turning to Monica. "You know how important feelings are. Aren't instincts and intuition usually right?"

"Oh please," Cara insisted, "life is about what you know, not what you feel. Even Monica's counseling work is based on science, just like everything else that actually works."

The two of them looked to Monica, awaiting a response.

Monica thought for a moment and then admitted, "To be perfectly honest, I'm a new resident, and I don't think I'm familiar enough with these candidates or their platforms to weigh in yet, but I'm sure you both have reasons why you support who you support."

"That's a cop-out," Frank said.

"And the middle-ground fallacy," added Cara.

"Not at all," Monica insisted, "I will eventually form my own opinion, and regardless of what that opinion ends up being, I'm sure I'll have points from both candidates that I agree and disagree with. That's not taking the middle ground, that's just the reality of living in a complicated world."

Neither teacher seemed satisfied with Monica's position, but she wasn't about to jump into something as complicated and divisive as politics without reviewing all the information and considering how she really thought and felt about all of it. She understood life was nuanced, and that polarized thinking was not going to work as a way forward for anyone. She wanted to tell them this idea but could see that they were both wrapped up in the situation. Monica decided to de-escalate the situation a little bit by bringing them back to the idea that they were all on the same team.

Monica said, "All of us are on the same team, and as teachers you're probably the best sources I could hope to have.

And it sounds like both of you are able to be honest and speak your minds."

"Yeah," Frank admitted, sounding a little less defensive, "we have some pretty good debates."

"It's true. Even when Frank is wrong—and he is—at least he's honestly wrong," Cara shot.

Frank rolled his eyes. "Typical. See, this is why we need a leader with *feelings* to unite the county, and not some sociopathic calculator."

"Dr. Spocard has studied politics her whole life. She's the only logical choice."

"James Dirk is a captain! That's real leadership experience! How much leadership experience can you get from reading a book?"

It was clear that these two were truly identifying with their candidates, and that they weren't particularly interested in collaborating or hearing out the other at that moment. They carried on like that for a while, and Monica spent some time listening to them. When lunch was over, she thanked them each for their thoughts.

"It's good that we're talking about this," Monica pointed out, "because all of us in education have to stick together."

"We are!" Frank agreed.

Cara didn't appear to hear the comment, as she was checking her phone and getting up.

"Good chatting with you," Cara said, without looking up.

Frank shook his head as Cara left, and after she had gone he said, "Can you believe that? She's so emotionally cut off she wasn't even here in the conversation."

"Maybe," Monica conceded, "but maybe something urgent came up too, you know? We don't know what that text said."

"Hm, fair enough," Frank agreed, "but back in my day we used to make eye contact. We'd actually listen to each other, and I don't feel that way anymore."

Monica realized that Frank had begun to assume the worst intentions with Cara, rather than give her the benefit of the doubt. She also recognized that Frank was easily put into a defensive posture. She knew that in order to get Frank to hear her, she'd need to find a way to connect to the idea that he had just presented.

Admittedly, Frank's comment made Monica feel a little bit defensive, herself. She understood that phones were often a social barrier, and she didn't particularly like the way they dominated everyone's attention either, but she felt at least that she and her peers were making an effort to mitigate that trend.

She realized she was identifying as the opposition to Frank's comment, even though part of her agreed with it. Monica didn't need to identify with her phone. She decided to identify with the truth that she could find in Frank's statement, which she believed was the message: human connection is important.

"I definitely enjoy my own life more when I focus on connecting with other people," Monica said.

"See, you get it!" Frank exclaimed. "All this technology and whatnot . . . it's not good for us. We're supposed to be out and about, bopping around in nature, building things, getting our hands dirty, playing games, all that good stuff. When I was a kid, we used to go out into these fields behind my house and just catch bugs. We found some weird ones!"

"Life is for living," Monica said.

"Well put. Well put. I wish people still thought that way."

Monica saw her opportunity to try to expand the connection.

"Honestly, I think that's how most of us in the school system feel," Monica said. "I've seen a lot of teachers making an effort to offer their students a chance to be more hands-on. We have an opportunity to show the next generation how to engage with the world they live in."

Monica wasn't sure if she was really phrasing her point the way she wanted to, but she also knew that sometimes it took a while to find a rhythm in communication with new people. She could tell Frank wanted to be a team player but didn't necessarily feel like he was part of the team. She wanted him to know that, indeed, they were all on a team together, and she felt like she had largely gotten that point across.

But just to be sure she added, "We're all on the same team, Frank."

Frank looked like he was about to send a knee-jerk response. Monica could feel the impulse in him to focus on the problem, and she was fully prepared for him to continue to list grievances, if that was what he needed at that moment, but to her surprise he sat back for a second and paused.

At last he said, "Same team. Yes indeed. That's very true. It's been good chatting with you."

"Likewise."

Frank put his hand out for a handshake, and Monica met his offer. His handshake was decisive and enthusiastic, the way that characters from old TV shows used to shake hands; it had a "good neighbor" quality to it.

As the two of them went their separate ways, Monica was glad she had caught herself before she had reacted in a defensive way. Frank didn't mean any harm to her, even if he presented things in a way that might seem to be criticism. He simply wanted to get everyone on board the same train of thought that he was on, because he felt deeply connected to his values and ideals.

Still, Monica could see how Frank's communication style could rub Cara the wrong way, and vice versa.

*Monica's Journal*

*Emil Harker on Influence*

- *As a school leader you are in a unique position to influence the lives of students and staff, which in turn impacts our overall community.*
- *We want to build a society in which people can work through differences in a collaborative way!*

# CHAPTER SIX

# BURNT OUT

Monica was exhausted. The first two weeks had been a nonstop sprint. She was pushing hard, but progress had not shown itself yet. Monica knew that improvements in school culture sometimes took a while to show themselves. She was looking forward to the weekend, since Mike had organized a little getaway for them.

"Nothing big or special," he had told her, "just a little weekend breather since I know how hard you've been working."

Monica was grateful for Mike's capacity to surprise her with spontaneous acts of love and caring, like the one she was looking forward to now. She recalled a time before she had realized the power of gratitude when she used to think of him as aloof and poorly organized. She had realized, as she examined her own perspectives, that this was only a narrative that she had been telling herself, and that his ability to improvise was a complimentary skill set that she needed.

In the same way, she brought orderliness and organization to the relationship, which Mike learned to cherish as well.

But that was for the future, and Monica needed to be in the present. She was about to meet Ms. Diane Flynn for the first time. Diane had been out sick for the first two weeks of school but was finally ready to return to work. The students in her class were vocal about their excitement for her return, and Principal Shore had described Diane as a "star teacher" on more than one occasion. Other teachers sang praises about how helpful and knowledgeable she was. It was the one thing Cara and Frank had immediately agreed on.

"She's great," Frank had said, "teaches from the heart."

"A highly intelligent human being," Cara had declared. "Yes, I agree; she has a good heart."

Monica was excited to meet such a positive force, and she honestly needed it. The previous counselor had left a lot of work undone, and it had fallen on Monica to pick up the slack. She was looking forward to a little boost from a fellow culture-builder.

Monica spotted Diane from down the hall. She was dressed in a pair of loose-fitting jeans and a sweatshirt, which had a coffee stain on it. Her hair was pulled back in a hasty ponytail, and she had dark circles under her eyes. She was leaning against the wall next to her classroom and didn't greet any of the kids passing by. In fact, she didn't even seem to notice Monica as she approached.

"Hi, I'm Monica," Monica announced with her hand extended out enthusiastically.

"Diane." The reply was flat and came with a reluctant handshake.

"I've heard a lot of good things," Monica said. "I'm happy to meet you."

"Yup." Diane put up a brief, half smile that didn't reach her eyes.

Monica was instantly hurt and disappointed. She wondered if she had done something wrong, or if she had come on too strong. Maybe she had forgotten to do something to help Diane out, or maybe Diane just didn't like her "vibe." She was transported back into her own days of high school when she was too awkward to fit into any of the cliques. She remembered how the cool girls had always ignored her when she would talk. Diane reminded her of them. They used to lean against the wall with the same disinterested look.

She stood there for a moment, not sure what to say. Diane wasn't even looking at her, but around her, down the hall.

"Well, it's nice to meet you." Monica managed to get that much out.

Even as she said it, she could tell it was that same, desperate "notice me" tone that she used to employ all those years ago.

"Uh huh."

*What is the deal here?* Monica wondered for a second.

She felt so alienated. Why was she feeling so destabilized by this stranger? Had she not done the work to hold her own self-sovereignty? She needed to pause for a second. To take a step back.

Monica turned away from Diane and cast her gaze down the hall in the other direction. She focused outwards, on the kids scurrying about in their own microcosm. *That's all these places are*, Monica thought, *just microcosms and subdivisions.*

She realized what was happening. She understood in an instant what it was that she was doing. *I'm making assumptions*, she realized to herself, *based on the limited perspective that I have in this tiny little subdivision of reality. There are a million things that could be going on to have Diane behaving this way, and me assuming that I'm the reason she's down is just my ego grasping at straws. She might still be recovering from her cold, or she might be tired from having to change her sleep cycle back to school time, or maybe there's some other stress going on. Calm down, Monica, remember what you learned from her old counseling professor, Dr. Eberts: Give people the benefit of the doubt. Don't assume.*

Having realized that Diane's demeanor probably had nothing to do with her, Monica pivoted into connecting rather than focusing on herself. She realized she hadn't even truly *received* Diane's answers. Sure, she had heard them, but if she was really honest, she had been so fixated on herself and how she felt that she had failed to give her attention to the teacher.

Monica leaned against the wall next to Diane, watching the students as they went by. For a minute they just stood there in silence.

"Today's been kind of tough?" Monica eventually asked, focusing her attention completely on Diane and trying to drop the admission as casually as possible.

Diane seemed to detect that Monica had turned her attention toward her rather than inward. People, Monica knew, could sense it when you were truly hearing them.

"You have no idea," Diane answered, with hardly any inflection at all.

"Some days are like that," Monica agreed, matching Diane's tone.

"Even in Australia," Diane added, flatly.

"Even in Australia?"

"It's from a book," Diane said.

"Gotcha," Monica nodded.

More silence. Monica accepted the silence.

"Well, do you feel like talking about it or should I let it be for now?" Monica asked.

"Eh . . . I'm not exactly feeling up to it," Diane said.

"No sweat," Monica said.

She watched as the river of students slowed into a trickling stream. The few stragglers hurried to get to their classrooms on time. The way the students rushed down the hall, awkwardly wielding their backpacks and precariously balancing their books reminded Monica that these were just kids, and that the world was big and fast and confusing and scary. She felt for them and remembered how hard it was to be a kid.

"It's hard to be a kid," Monica noted without even realizing she was saying it out loud.

"It is," Diane agreed. "It's really, really hard, and nobody understands."

The last of the students trickled in. Class was ready to begin again. Another hour to another day in another year was starting, like a clock hand shifting past the threshold of one moment into the next.

"Well," Monica said, standing up straight again, "I'm looking forward to working with you."

"Sure thing," Diane said, standing up herself, "and likewise."

Diane turned into her classroom, and Monica started back down the hall. The bell rang, indicating class had officially begun.

Monica didn't feel great about the exchange, but she also didn't feel as run down as she had beforehand. She knew that she had approached with an artificial positivity, when in truth she had been feeling burnt out herself. Diane had been grumpy, sure, but at least she had been authentic in her grumpiness. The exchange had been therapeutic, despite its brevity and overcast tone.

By the time Monica had returned to her office, she was feeling perfectly neutral about the exchange, which was a bit of an improvement. A bit of an improvement, Monica knew, was all anyone could ever ask for.

---

*Monica's Journal*

*Dr. Pete Getz on Being a School Leader*

- *A good school leader needs to know that changes on campus will negatively impact some staff members.*
  - *Be able to recognize this struggle and give them support during it.*
  - *If a teacher is struggling, we need to realize it is a big deal for that person.*

## Dr. Stephanie Eberts on Engaging Teachers

- Look at school culture first and determine how this teacher is not connected to it.
- Try to figure out what the problem is in the system that is affecting that teacher.
- Work to see if this is something that can be worked on in collaboration.
- Showing this teacher respect can help revitalize them.
- Realize that sometimes, in some situations, teachers need a vacation, a break, or maybe even a transfer to a different school.

# CHAPTER SEVEN

# GOLFMAST3R_ DAD3288

With eyes closed, Dale softly counted to four in his mind as he took in a deep, slow breath. He held his breath for another four-count before finally exhaling with that same mental note of *One, two, three, four.* When the exhale had finished, he counted to four once more before moving on to his next breath.

Dale had learned about breathing squares when he was still a student. He had learned them from Mr. Lohrman, a patient and peculiar man with a dopey grin and glasses with lenses so thick that he gave off a cartoonish impression, despite his intellectual brilliance. Mr. Lohrman was the one who ran chess club at Dale's school back then, and he had recognized Dale's struggle to keep his anxiety under control. Now, as a teacher himself, Dale had shared the idea with many of his own students. It was a simple tool, but it had changed Dale's life, and he hoped to pay it forward to the next generation just as Mr. Lohrman had.

The glow of Dale's computer was waiting for him when he opened his eyes, and he reread the exchange between himself and the parent that had been a thorn in his side over the past few days.

GOLFMAST3R_DAD3288: Honestly this just seems like a load of BS. Do you realize they take 30% of the money they raise? That doesn't sound like charity to me, that sounds like exploitation.

MrDale42: I hear your concern, but it's common practice to use some of the funds raised for the organization itself. They have to make money, too.

GOLFMAST3R_DAD3288: Are you getting kickbacks from them??? Because it sounds like you're really on their side here. As for me, I'm on the side of our kids, and I think we— THE PARENTS—are owed transparency so if they're paying you to promote their program I think it's only fair for us to know now.

MrDale42: No, I'm not getting any kickbacks from them. I'm simply stating that these charities need to pay for their own expenses.

GOLFMAST3R_DAD3288: Charities? Last time I checked companies that make a profit aren't charities. Man, they're really taking you for a ride, buckaroo. Tell you what, I've got a bridge in Florida I'd like to sell you. Can't you see how naive you're being? These guys are coming in here, "raising money" and taking a third of it? What do they even do anyway? Last I checked it's our kids out there knocking on doors and getting people to give up their cash. Meanwhile they give out some cheap plastic whistles and crappy books.

MrDale42: They give out way more than that.

GOLFMAST3R_DAD3288: Way to miss my point, Dale. This is a SCAM. I'm amazed, truly. I'm baffled. OPEN YOUR EYES.

MrDale42: I don't think this conversation is serving either of us at this point.

GOLFMAST3R_DAD3288: Typical! Rather than address the points I bring up, you want to run. The parents aren't just going to sit back while our kids get used by these greedy snakes. Our voices will be HEARD.

MrDale42: You're making a big deal out of something that isn't.

GOLFMAST3R_DAD3288: See? It's that sort of wishy-washy, weak-stomached abdication of responsibility that has this country in the mess it's in. You teachers are so insulated from the real world that you never have to develop your COMMON SENSE. No wonder education in America is going down the toilet.

Dale's cat, Patches, jumped onto the keyboard, interrupting Dale's response. The abrupt intrusion startled Dale into the realization of what he was doing in that moment. He realized how childish this exchange was getting, and that he did not owe any reply to this parent. What was he doing wasting his Saturday arguing on the Internet?

"Thanks, Patches."

The cat squinted with delight as Dale scratched behind the little Singapura's ears. Dale set his computer aside and leaned back on his couch. What was it about this guy that drew him into such ridiculous arguments? Why was he wasting his time trying to defend the district's decision to use an organization that consistently raised $30,000 a year for the school?

Patches flopped onto Dale's stomach, basking in the attention.

"I'm very silly sometimes, Patches," Dale told his cat, "not always, but definitely sometimes."

"Mrrrow," the cat chirped, as if in agreement.

"There are better uses of my time, aren't there, buddy?"

Without warning, the cat hopped up and leapt from the couch, playfully ducking and dodging across the cluttered floor on his way toward the kitchen. Somehow he managed to dodge all the books, journals, and pens that Dale had scattered across the ground.

Dale looked across the room at the analog clock his roommate had built, which featured a garden gnome with a red hat and sunglasses pointing out the time. It was exactly 11:30 a.m., so the gnome looked like it was striking a disco pose. Dale realized if he left now, he could walk down to the cafe and catch a game or two at the local chess meet up.

He got up and followed Patches into the kitchen. To express his gratitude, he took a sardine out from the fridge and fed it to the tiny carnivore.

"You're a real one, Patches," Dale said.

The cat gobbled up the fish while the teacher threw on his jacket and slipped on his shoes, which he kept perpetually loose enough to slide on while never needing to be tied and untied. Dale stepped out the door and went on his way.

For the first few blocks, he considered how he'd respond to GOLFMAST3R_DAD3288, but his mind soon departed from that line to the possibility of playing against his greatest rival. Before long he was immersed in the endless combinations of openings and tactics of his favorite game, so that by the time he arrived, the ridiculous online argument held no place in his consciousness. Of the past seven games against his opponent, each had ended in a draw. If he was to win, he needed a clear head in the present moment.

As Dale stepped into the cafe, he was greeted by his chess nemesis.

"Well, well, well . . . look who decided to turn up. You've got some guts showing your face here again after that embarrassing blunder last week, Dale."

"I still forced the stalemate, didn't I? And that's Mr. Dale to you, Norbert."

"Ha, we aren't in school. Out here in the real world you're just another pleb."

*Go ahead. Lean into that hubris,* Mr. Dale thought, taking his seat.

Dale had met aggressive sorts like Norbert and GOLF MAST3R_DAD3288 all his life. They had a tendency to assume they were right even when they didn't know the whole situation. Dale didn't want to fall into the same trap and preferred to assume the posture of the underdog.

Norbert opened with e4, confidently sliding his king's pawn toward the center of the board.

Dale decided to use Norbert's pride to his advantage. *The Pirc Defense will give him a false sense of security,* he thought to himself, *he'll never even realize he's doing exactly what I want.*

Dale moved his queen's pawn up just one square. Norbert's overconfidence escalated in seeing such a "small" move. Dale did his best to contain his joy. He took in a slow breath, held it, and exhaled again. *One, two, three, four.*

# CHAPTER EIGHT

# RETREAT AND REFOCUS

Monica was happy to have arrived at the extended Labor Day weekend. Mike had gotten the two of them a little cabin for the next three days. It was tucked away a few miles into the hills. She had enjoyed the twists and turns of the dirt road that led there and had been particularly enchanted by the silence of nature that had become so apparent the moment they had parked.

"You hear that?" Monica asked Mike.

Mike stood still for a moment, listening carefully. He realized what she was getting at, and smiled back at her, warmly. Monica gave him a nod that said *You did good getting this place.*

Monica had explained to Mike that she would have to bring some of her work with her, but that it wouldn't dominate the trip. She knew she needed to communicate that need for time up front in order to give a reasonable expectation for the weekend.

"I'll try to get it done on day one so that we can enjoy the other two days together," Monica had told him. Mike had agreed that that was alright with him, and that he would spend the first day hiking.

"I could use a little time alone out in nature myself," he had said.

After they had unpacked, Monica brewed herself a cup of tea. The cabin had a large enough desk for her to lay out her materials, and before long she was in comfortable sweatpants and a T-shirt with a warm mug of green tea in her hand.

"Alright, I'm about to head out," Mike told her. "Anything else before I go?"

This was exactly what Monica had needed: space and time away from both the school and her home. Here was a location that had no emotions or obligations attached. She could think clearly here. She was grateful that Mike had taken the initiative. He probably didn't even really realize how much of a bull's-eye he had hit by planning this little trip.

"Nope, I'm all set, except," she kissed him on the cheek, "thank you. This is exactly what I needed."

It never ceased to amaze her how tiny a demonstration of gratitude it took to make Mike bask in his victory.

"You're very welcome," Mike said, beaming. "I'll see you in . . . I don't know how long, but I'll see you later!"

With that, he bounded out the door with a youthful energy that always came to the surface when he was out in nature.

Monica turned back to her desk and sipped her tea as she looked over her workstation. Her journal and a handful of notes were laying on the desk. Altogether, she was sure she now had enough information to create a plan of action. She had set intentions and had done those tasks that generally help a school, but now that she had a feel for this particular school, she was ready to outline a few of her ideas.

She picked up her pen and began outlining action steps for each one of her notes.

## Monica's Journal

### Notes and Observations on the School

- Principal Shore—Hannah
  - Team player, positive
  - Overworked
  - Attacks from parents? Demanding staff?
    - She mentioned in passing that she felt like the "emotions police."

ACTION STEP: Give Hannah space to talk. Try to find time when she can speak her mind.

- Betty reached out about a student named Tony Sharkley.
  - Tony has a lot of disciplinary notes.
    - I have greeted him a few times in the hall, but response is limited.

ACTION STEP: Should meet with Betty, then possibly Tony.

- *Kids are on phones a lot! Too much.*
  - *Peer-to-peer programming and mindfulness can help.*
  - *Also, boundaries on phone use are needed.*
  - *Maybe consider a new school-wide policy on phones.*

*ACTION STEPS: Help teachers on strategies to get kids off phones; start a peer-to-peer program.*

- *Cara and Frank got into it in the hall; the argument got pretty heated.*
  - *I don't really care for either candidate, to be honest.*

*ACTION STEPS: Focus on connecting them with common ground.*

- *Ms. Diane Flynn—seems unhappy!*
  - *Checked in a second time, still unhappy, didn't want to talk.*

> ∘ *At this point I need to find a way to get her to tell me what's bothering her so I can offer support/solutions.*
>
> *ACTION STEPS: It's time to find out what's up, schedule meetup (no pressure!).*
>
> • *Dale came by my office yesterday asking me how to handle a conflict with a parent regarding a fundraiser? I need details.*
>
> *ACTION STEP: Meet with him to talk about it.*

Monica was excited to use these conflicts to teach the school the best practices for resolution that she had learned. She knew that most of these conflicts would unfold organically, in due time and without much of a push on her part. She didn't want to rush connections. It was best to let those things happen at their normal pace, and to simply recognize opportunities as they occurred.

What she could take initiative on, however, was creating a peer-to-peer program to start to steer the school's culture toward success and positivity.

Her next step was to ask teachers to scout for good candidates for that program. She knew that a wide range of students would be best, and that student leaders were often found in surprising places.

She outlined the cliques that she had observed in the school, making sure not to overlook any group that she had identified. The best way to get students to succeed, she knew, was to get them to buy in and have ownership of the school. She knew that most students would participate if given the chance.

The outlook of the school was still somewhat chaotic in her mind. She realized she had a map but was still not familiar with the territory it represented. Connection was obviously the next step, but she would need to really focus on the specific tools she had learned throughout her career to influence the conflicts she had identified to solutions that served everyone.

And of course, as she had learned alongside Mike, it isn't just about finding a resolution to the conflict; it's also about *how* you do it.

Monica had laid the groundwork for connection. Now it was time to get specific.

# CONNECTION

# CHAPTER NINE

# A LITTLE NOW OR A LOT LATER

Monica's notes had already taken up the majority of her new notebook. She reviewed the situations in the school that needed, she believed, to be addressed.

It felt good to have a lay of the land, and to have an idea of what the main conflicts in her school were. Although some of the specifics were still illusive, she had a pretty good feeling about the school, and the people in it. On the whole, the people in the school meant well, but there was always a certain tension in the air.

Monica concluded that the school's culture was so dedicated to staying positive that they failed to address, or even acknowledge, the conflicts that they were experiencing.

Monica had seen this before. In fact, it was one of the most common problems she had encountered in both school settings and corporate settings. She chalked it up largely to the idea that very few people wanted to rock the boat unless things went so badly that it was intolerable for them. The members of the school believed in positivity. They wanted to be positive and to be seen as positive. The "logic" for some schools is that part of positivity is avoiding things that are perceived as negative, such as conflict.

Monica knew that this was a mistake, even though it came from a place of good intentions. Her own marriage had proven to her that an essential part of every relationship was to embrace conflict, despite the short-term negative feelings it might impose in the immediate moment.

As the saying goes, "You can either pay a little now, or a lot later." This was true for many things, but Monica knew it was especially true for discomfort in relationships.

There had been a time when she had, more or less, attempted the same tactic of avoidance. She and Mike were, at the time, going through the rough patch mentioned earlier. She thought that maybe it was all her fault that things were not working, and that she just needed to "be more positive." As a result, she folded on every issue that came up, and tried to let everything go.

The outcome was not at all what she hoped. Deep down, Mike knew something was wrong, and so did she. Resentment for him began to build, but with no way for him to understand or navigate it. Her positive vibes collapsed against the resentment, and she began to snap at him regularly. This confused and hurt him, since he didn't understand which of her needs weren't being met.

Finally, Monica realized that the conflict existed *until it was resolved.* No amount of ignoring it would make it go away. If she brushed it to the side, it still existed. If she delayed it or tried to change the topic, it still existed. The only way to dispel the conflict was to face it. Once it was addressed, it was gone.

She and Mike changed their tactic, with the help of their marriage counselor, to addressing conflict in a productive way.

"The sooner it's done, the sooner we get back to good times," Monica realized and explained to Mike one day, "but *how* it's done is also very important, because that creates the good times."

She leaned back in her chair, reflecting on the teachers who had shown her the way and on the simple concepts that had driven virtually all her success as a counselor. She knew each of the problems the school faced could be resolved and that she had the tools to do so. She kept those tools handy and would review them before the upcoming encounters.

One last time she looked over her journal, which contained all the relevant advice for each of the conflicts she had outlined. It was all there. The plan was outlined. More importantly, she felt recharged and ready to go.

*Monica's Journal*

*Dr. Pete Getz on Self-Care*

- *Practice self-care and a healthy balance between work and personal life.*
  - *Find things in your life that you enjoy and go do them.*

# CHAPTER TEN

# SILLY BEANS

"You can call me Hannah, by the way," Principal Shore said as she settled into the big, soft, purple sofa that Monica had put in her office. "We're on a team, you know?"

"Totally," Monica agreed.

Monica and Hannah had slowly built a rapport over the past few weeks. Despite her busy workload, Monica had made it her ambition to regularly touch base with everyone working at the school. During that time, Monica had compiled notes on the different conflicts that she had noticed throughout the school. She knew the power of journaling, and that the advice she had gotten from her teachers and peers throughout her education would prove useful as she tried to improve the relationships in her school through positive conflict resolution.

Hannah, it seemed, was already ready to open up about her problems. Monica had not even prompted her to do so, but merely made it clear that she was always available to talk. It made sense, since Hannah had already demonstrated on an almost daily basis that she highly valued communication, and clearly understood that part of leadership was allowing herself and others to be vulnerable. Those qualities had been a massive factor in Monica deciding to work at Serenity Springs.

"I feel like the job is . . . not the same as when I started," Hannah admitted. "Half of what I do is policing social media and the feelings of students. I feel like I can't even help them or give them practical or useful advice, because I truly don't feel safe speaking my mind about a lot of these issues. The parents are so quick to attack these days, and everything is politicized. *Everything*. It seems like politics has invaded every nook and cranny in the world. Did you know we had parents who were upset at the orange juice company we were using because the CEO of the company had made campaign donations to–I don't even know–some politician. I don't follow that stuff, really. I just want to help *this* community. I don't even consider myself a political person, but I feel like if I step on people's toes, I'll get crucified. And then there's the school board, they have no idea what's actually happening in these schools. I really want to help fix things, but it just feels like there's no way to get through to them. They just don't understand. How could they? I don't blame them; they live in an entirely different world. I've seen glimpses of it, and it's brutal! If I knew half of what they were dealing with, I probably wouldn't even complain about them. Sorry, I don't mean to dump all of this on you."

"It's okay," Monica replied, "we all need to talk through our problems. That's how a team works."

"I'm glad you're here. You understand the most important thing. We're all on a team, truly. Not just in this school. Human beings. We're all trying to do good things. That's why it's so frustrating to feel like I have to be so . . . corporate? Restrained? I don't even know what the right word is. I definitely don't feel like I can be myself, it's like I have to constantly censor myself. Sometimes it's like, 'Yeah, the bus schedule isn't perfect for everyone, but do you have any idea how many kids we are moving around on a daily basis? Is it really worth getting angry, calling me first thing in the morning, and shouting at me?' And as a human being I'm thinking, 'Wow, you can't even handle the bus taking seven minutes more to get your kid home? How do you suck that bad at life? And how dare you come at me like that? And hasn't anyone taught you how to have a conversation as an adult?' But as a principal, I have to smile, listen, and then try to pretend to look for solutions to a problem that I know we've already tried to solve to the best of our abilities."

Monica couldn't help but chuckle at the absurdity of the bus situation, "Yeah, that's . . ."

"It's frickin' silly, man!" Hannah chuckled as well.

"It *is* frickin' silly!" Monica exclaimed.

The two of them looked at each other, nodding and announced in unison, "It's frickin' silly!"

The mutual laughter that followed wasn't particularly loud, or overwhelming, but it was bubbly enough to offer some relief from the day for both of them. For a moment they both felt fun again.

"Ah, yeah . . . that's the good stuff," Hannah said. "It feels good to be a human being."

"My niece," Monica said, "always says beans instead of beings. She says, 'Aunt Monica, we are human beans.'"

"Frickin' silly human beans," Hannah concluded. "Ahhh, well thanks for letting me vent. What are your thoughts on all of that? Any advice?"

Monica thought for a moment and then said, "All we can do when things are this way is to accept the reality of our situation and ask ourselves what we can do given that reality."

"I think I'm still in the process of accepting the reality of my situation, to be honest."

"Yeah," Monica observed, "I think given how quickly things are changing, that makes sense."

"But at the same time, I do see how that's true. Even the thought is kind of empowering," Hannah said.

"It definitely is," Monica agreed, "because from that place, we can make meaningful decisions."

"Thanks Monica," Hannah said as she got up.

Monica smiled and said, "I'm happy to help."

---

*Monica's Journal*

*Tamara Givens on Maintaining Enthusiasm*

- *We have to remember why we got into education in the first place.*
  - *Life is a journey, not a destination.*
  - *We can get through everything eventually.*
  - *Always remember what is best for the kids.*

- Focus on building relationships with staff above all else.
  - This gives admins a group of people who can support them and help them not feel alone.
  - The team is what can give you the personal energy to move forward.

## Emil Harker on Redefining Reality

- It is important to define and accept our reality.
- Come to a point where you can accept this new reality.
- Use this new reality to change your perspective on your job or your idea of success.
  - The new paradigm shift will create motivation and energy.

# CHAPTER ELEVEN

# TRULY TROUBLED TONY

"Tony's outbursts have escalated. I've tried everything. He can't even have a civilized discussion. I've got a class to teach, and he's actively preventing that from happening. I'm out of ideas here," said Betty.

Betty was calm at the moment, but Monica could see that this was someone who had exhausted her patience completely. There was no denying it, Tony's folder had a disturbing number of reported behavioral issues.

"So that's why I scheduled this meeting," Betty continued, "to see if you have any ideas on how to handle it because at this point, it's starting to look like I simply cannot keep my class running with him in it."

Monica nodded, recalling her objective: connect first, correct second.

"Wow!" Monica considered how exhausting it must be to deal with that sort of behavior day after day and said, "I'm just imagining what it must be like to deal with that and honestly, that must be hell."

"It is!" Betty sounded relieved to have someone understand. "And the thing that peeves me the most is that it takes away from other students who actually *want* to learn math."

"Yeah, the situation is absolutely not fair to anyone in that classroom, including you," Monica agreed.

"Thank you!" Betty put her hands up in the air to emphasize her gratitude.

"So let me ask you, what needs to be done?"

Betty shrugged. "I don't know, I guess ... honestly, I just don't think I have the . . . resources to accommodate him. I hate to say it but he's one of those kids who–and I'm not judging him–he just doesn't fit in with the other normal . . ."

Betty caught herself. She had nearly implied that Tony was not normal. She immediately felt concerned that Monica would judge her for her almost politically incorrect state-ment. She had been trying her best to present everything in the most sanitized language possible, but she just couldn't keep from slipping back into her normal register.

"Don't worry," Monica assured her, "you can speak plainly in this room. I'm not about to get upset with you for being direct. In fact, I'd honestly rather just speak plainly."

Betty hesitated for a moment and then confessed, "Honestly, I want that little punk out of my class. He's preventing the other kids from learning, and it's simply not fair to them."

Monica took a second to consider the situation. It was clear that Betty was open to any help she could get, but it was equally clear she had truly done everything she knew how to do. She wanted Betty to try the method of "connect first, correct second" but also knew that she needed to offer an escape plan as well if that didn't work.

"Alright. I think I understand the situation," Monica began, "and I have a few ideas, but I want to workshop them with you since you're the one who knows what's really happening best. Sound good?"

"For sure! Let's hear it," Betty agreed.

"Okay," Monica continued, "I can clearly see that you've truly tried with Tony, but we've obviously got a kid with major behavioral issues, so I want to state up front that realistically, he truly might need to get the help he requires from a different program or person. Now, what that looks like is up to him, because ultimately he's going to either decide to meet the standards of your classroom, or not."

Betty leaned in. She had never, in her career as a teacher, had anyone in administration simply agree with her assessment without putting in their own two cents. It was true, she had done everything she knew to do, and she'd learned a lot in her 15 years as a math teacher.

"So I think it's time to let him know that's what he's facing," Monica concluded. Then she added, "But I have to ask, do you think there's any chance he'll recognize he doesn't want that outcome and get in line?"

Betty shrugged, "I truly don't know at this point."

"I want to be clear: I'm not telling you what I think we should do. I'm asking for your opinion as an education professional. Do you think this kid has a chance at all?"

"I see. Okay then . . . let me think." Betty took a long moment to reflect on the question. "As angry as I am, I do think there's a chance."

"Are you open to hearing how I'd go about that?"

"Sure," Betty looked skeptical, but engaged.

"Great," said Monica, "I think it would be a good idea to look at it as a two-step process. Step one: connect with him. It sounds like he arrives in a defensive space pretty often. So start with relating to him. Something like, 'Hey, I need your help. See, I need to do my job and teach this class. Now I know you must have reasons for how you feel in class. I don't know what your reasons are, but I'm guessing this year is pretty tough, is that right?'"

Betty nodded. "Okay, I see what you're doing with that. Get him to drop his guard."

"Exactly. He needs to know it's not a confrontation," Monica agreed, "so then he might open up, or he might turtle up. That's up to him, but you're sending the signal: I am on your team. If he opens up, maybe you'll learn more about his situation. Maybe he'll tell you his motives, and maybe you two can move forward. Either way, after you hear him out, you move on to step two, which is to correct his behavior."

"Cool. How would you do that?"

"I'd say something like, 'I really want to provide support for you, so we can talk things over if you're having a tough day, or if you need to take a minute outside of class, we can set up a code word and you can step outside to take a little time for yourself . . . but if that doesn't work, then I have to be honest, that means I might not be able to provide the support you need right now. And I want you to get the support you need so that might mean looking for that support elsewhere. If that's what you need, that's okay. If you don't need that and you can follow the class standards, that's okay too. Ultimately, it's your choice. I just want to make sure you understand the choice you'll be making."

"Got it. Connect, and then correct. Easy," Betty nodded.

"Yup. It's best to keep it simple because if he gets emotional, you only need to remember to connect, and when he's good and stable, that's when you're free to make the correction. After that, you can send him to come see me, because I'd also like to discuss his behavior in other classes as well."

Monica could see that Betty was already connecting to the idea in her mind. The simple concept was effortless for the veteran teacher to grasp. It was clear that she was already implementing the idea into her teaching toolbelt.

"You've used this before?" Betty asked. "It works?"

"I have, and it usually does," Monica confirmed. "If you're interested in my notes, I can get them for you. I learned the technique from Emil Harker. He wrote a book called *You Can Turn Conflict into Closeness* that you'd probably like."

"Thank you," Betty considered the upcoming weekend. She had a lot of space for the first time in a long time over the next two days. She wanted to approach Monday as her best self, to give the best possible attempt at helping Tony. Sure, he was a pain, but she couldn't help but want him to succeed. Betty wanted all her kids to succeed. It was simply part of her nature, and it was the reason she had become a teacher in the first place.

"When I was little, I was an absolute punk," Betty told Monica. "I used to skip school to smoke cigarettes under the bleachers—you know the type. I didn't like authority because I realized early on that most authority figures were just as wrong as everyone else. Just like Tony, I didn't see the point to school . . . until this one teacher, Ms. Lorenz, who just kind of decided to take me under her wing."

She paused there, reflecting on her own experiences, and how similar they were to Tony. She realized she had an opportunity to make an impact on him, the same way Ms. Lorenz had impacted her.

"It only takes one charismatic adult to turn a kid's life around," Monica said.

Betty nodded. A few cheesy responses ran through her head, but they were all just too gooey for her taste, so instead she said, "Thanks, Monica."

"No problem. Let's continue to work together on this. You can step into my office anytime, but let's also schedule a regular meeting so we can stay on the same page."

Betty agreed, and they arranged a handful of check-in times. After they had set up their plan, Betty left feeling much better about the whole situation.

After Betty had gone, Monica examined Tony's file. She noticed that almost all of his outbursts were associated with political or social commentary. Some of the points were, frankly, pretty spot on. He often ranted about the system and its imperfections, and Monica recognized that there was indeed a lot that needed to be fixed.

Maybe he would recognize the reality of the situation, that Betty was trying to help as a human being and not as an avatar of a system he hated. If so, he'd have a shot at turning a lot around. He was, after all, clearly a bright student. He had gotten solid grades until that year, and even with the growing list of disciplinary actions, he was maintaining a B average.

Her biggest concern was a footnote in one of the reports stating that he had been spending time during computer lab on a forum that Monica hadn't recognized. Clearly the teacher reporting it didn't know what the forum was either and hadn't really thought too much about it other than that it was getting in the way of Tony doing the work required for the class.

However, when Monica looked into the forum, she discovered it had some pretty intense content. A lot of what was discussed were extreme political ideas and cultural commentary, which she didn't see as bad in itself. After all, Monica reasoned, part of education is investigating all positions without attaching oneself to them. However, there was another side to the forum that was deeply troubling to her. It presented hateful and violent ideologies, and even encouraged extreme antisocial behavior.

One post in particular made her stomach drop. In it, one of the posters was celebrating a recent shooting that had taken place at a mall. Although other commenters quickly opposed and shut the thought down, they did so not as a moral opposition, but out of concern that the comment could draw unwanted attention to the forum.

```
STFU, dumbass! Do you want the hive
to learn about this place?
```

Monica knew enough about these forums to recognize that this "us versus them" mentality was dangerous, and that a student like Tony who felt disillusioned and disconnected was particularly susceptible to rhetoric that painted everyone outside of the group as bad. That sort of black-and-white, us-versus-them, we're-the-good-guys thinking, Monica knew, was a treacherous road for a young mind, and a commonly used tactic in cults and other problematic social groups.

What Tony needed was authentic connection—real people he could get to know, so that he could learn that the vast majority of people aren't evil at all.

Monica believed in Betty. She believed that she had the capacity to use Emil's simple tool to leverage her natural ability as a teacher to connect to this lost student. But if not, Monica knew, then they might indeed have to find a different place for Tony to go. They simply didn't possess the resources as a school to continue to support a student who couldn't function in a classroom.

She wasn't sure if he was a risk. It appeared that he hadn't commented in the forums and was only reading, or "lurking." Still, she wasn't about to sweep something like this under the rug.

She decided to start investigating alternatives, just in case. She picked up the phone to call one of her peers, a counselor who had specialized in helping troubled students. They had a plan, and both options were viable. Ultimately, it was up to Tony to decide his own path.

## Monica's Journal

### Emil Harker on Intent and Conflict

- Assume good intent in the reason the student is acting the way they are.
- Connect with the student before you correct.
- We need to rewire our idea of conflict and respond in a different way.
  - This is resolved by hijacking the impulsive desire to become defensive.
    - We can do this in four easy steps:
      1. Sharing our feelings and reasons in a vulnerable way.
      2. Using a transition statement such as, "but if I see it from your point of view" or "if I look at it from your angle."
      3. Then stating what you think it is like to be in the other person's shoes.
      4. And lastly checking in to see if you are right in stating how the person feels.

- Establish clear boundaries of what is expected in the class.
  - Let the student know that if they don't respect boundaries that something might have to change
    - And they will have to face consequences for their choices.
    - However, the likelihood of this should be low if there is a connection built into the relationship.

# CHAPTER TWELVE

# SERIOUS DIGITAL BEEF

"I don't want people to think I'm a tattle tale," Jennifer said, as she sat in front of Monica, "so you can't let anyone know I'm telling you this."

"I know you want confidentiality. We can do our best to protect that, but I just have to make sure everyone is safe," Monica said.

"Okay. I understand. Here's the deal: Sandra and Maya have been fighting online. Like, seriously fighting, and it's really not okay right now. They've been getting worse about it. They're both online being really nasty, and it's not even funny anymore. Plus they have a lot of followers now that are egging them on, and I just don't think that it's going to turn out well. I usually don't even care about online drama, but I feel like this is different. I think it's going to get worse, so that's why I'm telling you. I'm not even involved. I just thought you should know."

"Thank you for telling me," Monica said. "Can you show me what you mean?"

Jennifer took her phone out of her pocket and pulled up the app. It was one of the newer social media platforms, and although Monica was aware of it, she was not yet familiar with it. She couldn't help but feel exhausted from the endless invasion of social media into the lives of her students. These kids were born into a system that provided a tool that gave them virtually limitless social leverage and put them in front of all the consequences that go with that power. She recalled her own adolescence, and how many ridiculous things she had thought and said. She was deeply thankful that nobody had recorded her early, chaotic years and posted them online for the world to see. This was exactly the reason that she needed to build a program to teach kids how to use this technology responsibly.

Jennifer showed her the history of the communication between Sandra and Maya. It wasn't pretty. At first it began with a series of posts from Sandra that could have just been teasing, but they eventually escalated into more direct and hurtful language. Disturbingly, the nastier the content of the post, the higher the number of likes. The most recent one was particularly nasty:

```
Let's all agree that Maya
Is now a social pariah
```

A host of laughing emojis and thumbs up were attached to the post, along with such insightful comments as "Got her!" and "Daaaaaaang!"

Maya's page, on the other hand, had become very silent over the past two weeks. She had gone from commenting somewhat regularly about her activities in theater to nothing at all. Her most recent post simply read:

```
Ouch.
```

It was sad to see. Monica wondered why she hadn't picked up on this kind of conflict earlier.

"Have they been arguing at school?" Monica asked Jennifer.

"I don't think so. I don't even think they're in any classes together."

"Alright," Monica said, "thank you for sharing this with me. I'm going to address it, but I won't bring your name up. I do appreciate you looking out for your classmates, Jennifer, that's a very caring and mature thing to do."

"Thanks," Jennifer said, putting her phone away.

Jennifer was one of those rare students that somehow seemed to already understand that, in life, you have to just try to be good to others and make the best with the hand you're dealt. She was no stranger, Monica knew, to struggle. She had been through a lot of counseling outside of school as she had dealt with her diagnosis of epilepsy. She had been forced to deal with a difficult situation early in life and had cultivated resilience as a result.

"Hey, Jennifer, while I'm thinking about it," Monica said, "do you have any interest in helping me out with a program I want to start here? It's focused on creating positive culture, especially around social media. Essentially, you'd be going into the younger classes and teaching them some of the skills you've learned. I'm looking to get a handful of student leaders together so we can create this program together. Is that something you'd be interested in?"

"As long as it doesn't interfere with the astronomy club, I'm up for it."

"It won't," Monica said.

"Deal!" Jennifer hopped up and headed out. She would be a good candidate to help other kids learn to be slightly more responsible both online and in real life.

*Real life, what a strange concept,* Monica thought to herself.

Monica leaned back in her chair and rubbed her eyes. This was the hardest part of her job. She wished she could take cell phones away from every kid in school. The fact that all of them had access to these devices was madness to her. How could a 15-year-old kid possibly handle unsupervised access to the Internet? How could a kid navigate the chaotic world of social media? How could their parents and teachers keep up with it all?

Monica needed a minute. She stood up, closed her door, and collapsed in her comfy chair.

When she was a kid, saying something mean resulted in seeing the other kid's pain expressed on their face. Online, the only feedback you got for that sort of behavior was upvotes from strangers who only wanted to see the fight get worse.

*Okay,* she thought to herself, *you need to accept the situation. Lamenting the reality of the situation isn't going to get you anywhere. Technology is here and it's probably here to stay.*

She had already reached out to Jane, their school's computer science teacher, and had gotten a list of students who teachers had suggested could be good leaders. She needed to add Jennifer to that list.

She reviewed the outline of her peer-to-peer program. It included an outline of simple steps for resolving problems like the one Maya and Sandra were facing.

- Ask yourself:
  - Would I say this in person?
  - Would I want everyone I know to read this, including . . .
    - My parents?
    - My teachers?
    - My friends?
    - My future employer?
- When in doubt, talk it out, and give the benefit of the doubt.
- If you're not sure if you should post, wait a day.

If any of those standards had been taught to Sandra, this mess would have been over before it started, but the reality of the situation was that they hadn't been. Monica knew that even though what Sandra had been saying was nasty, the main problem was that she didn't understand what she was doing, and that she didn't understand the results of her actions.

But maybe there was a chance to do a lot of good here. Monica knew that if she could get Sandra and Maya to just talk out their situation, they would inevitably find understanding and resolve their problems. Maybe they'd be willing to teach the younger students what had happened to them so they wouldn't make the same mistake.

Thankfully, things hadn't escalated too far yet, but they needed to nip this in the bud straight away. Who knew when the next message would be sent or how much distress Sandra was really in. She decided to bring in Maya first so that she couldn't do anymore damage, and then coach her through the situation.

---

*Monica's Journal*

*Dr. Stephanie Eberts on Student Leadership and Social Media*

- *Consider giving the student a leadership role on campus or something that they can be a part of.*

- In doing this, they will feel cared for and seen.
  - Help the student find their tribe and connection on campus.
- Realize that adults have fully developed brains and students do not.
- Educate students and parents on the impacts of social media.
  - Use real-world stories of social media issues to educate kids about outcomes and consequences.
- Work to bring face-to-face student mediation into this type of situation.
  - Form mediation contracts with the students.

# CHAPTER THIRTEEN

# A LITTLE AD HOMINEM

The political battle between Cara and Frank had not ceased.

"Honestly, you're just being obtuse at this point," Cara announced. "You and Dirk have that in common."

"Again with the ad hominem attacks! I thought logic was your thing, and yet you can't open your mouth without a fallacy spilling out," Frank accused.

"You're intentionally missing the point. If you could set your fragile ego aside for one moment and actually consider the facts of the situation, you'd see that Spocard is the only reasonable choice."

"You're intolerable!"

"You're absurd!"

"You're a robot!"

"You're a buffoon!"

The halls were echoing with the argument between Cara and Frank, and Monica was happening by. They were making quite the scene, and students were starting to gather around the heated argument. Monica decided to go check it out.

By the time she arrived, the two teachers had come to their senses.

"The little show is over. Don't you have classes to get to?" Cara said, shooing the kids away.

Frank had his arms crossed and was looking pretty red in the face. Cara was clearly flustered too and trying not to take that frustration out on the kids. It was fifth hour, and Frank had to get to his class. He looked as though he had more to say but went inside his classroom instead.

Cara, however, had her planning hour and had some time to chat.

"Can you believe him?" Cara said to Monica when Frank left.

Cara's tone was defensive, even to Monica. Monica could tell that she was ready to shut out any opposition in *that* moment. She also knew a very useful concept that she'd learned over the course of her career: if you can get someone to start walking, you can get them to start talking.

"Sounded like a pretty heated argument," Monica noted. "Want to go for a walk and chat about it?"

"Yes, please. I need to vent."

The two of them walked down the hall and out the door.

Cara transformed the moment she was out the door. Although she was still tense, her shoulders seemed to relax and loosen up from the tight raised position they had been in just a few minutes ago. She let out a huge sigh as she walked.

"It's just so frustrating to deal with people who don't *think*," Cara said.

Monica knew that Cara was deciding how much to say, and that if she interrupted and weighed in, then Cara would close off again. She decided instead to offer Cara a little more space to vent. Now was the time to listen, not comment. At the same time, Monica didn't want to take sides, or give the impression that she thought Frank was doing anything wrong by holding the positions that he held. She needed to remain relaxed and neutral. *Remember, Monica,* she thought to herself, *you're all on the same team.*

"Yeah?" Monica prompted, being sure to intonate curiosity rather than agreement.

"Yeah," Cara continued, "there's just no reasoning with the man. He doesn't even seem to hear the points I'm making."

Monica noticed that Cara was making broad generalizations and wanted to try to tie her back to the immediate situation, rather than her overall perception of Frank. She knew Cara was capable of giving her own account of the conversation that had just happened, but that focusing on such wide statements would not lead to resolution and would only lead to confirming the conclusion she had already reached.

"Can you give an example?" Monica asked.

"I'm sure I could give a dozen!" Cara said. "So this recent conversation, we were talking about which candidate would have better judgment for policies surrounding education. I pointed out that Spocard has spent her whole life in education, so it would stand to reason that she would understand the ins and outs. Meanwhile, Dirk hasn't even been in a school since he graduated undergrad!"

"And what did Frank say?"

"He just ignored it, as usual. He said something about—I don't know—how schools used to be about human connection or something totally unrelated. He didn't even acknowledge the point I was making."

Monica saw the opportunity to begin to unify them.

"I can imagine how frustrating that would be. It sounds as though you both feel pretty passionately about how our government interacts with education."

"Ha, yeah, I guess we do," Cara admitted, "but he's just so focused on being right and petting his ego that he can't set it down long enough to really hear what I'm saying."

This was the point at which Monica had the chance to humanize Frank to Cara. It was clear that the two of them were very much attached and identifying with their own candidates, but that the point where they agreed was that the schools needed to be taken care of and guided by a caring and knowledgeable leader. The main issue was that the system itself had set them up to focus on their differences rather than their commonalities.

Cara was close to the truth, but still seeing the world through the reality distortion field of "us versus them" that was so prevalent these days. If she could just guide her to recognizing that they both wanted what was best, then

Cara would see that their disagreements weren't from being opposed, and actually came from both of them wanting the same thing.

However, she knew that people tend to get defensive when their ideas are opposed, so she needed to gently intercept the trajectory of the conversation by relating to Cara even as she prepared to disagree with her.

"I see the truth in what you're saying when you tell me that you don't feel heard. And I totally understand how that feeling can give you the impression that Frank is focused on just being right, but would you be interested in hearing a different point of view?"

By asking permission to share a different point of view, Monica was handing over agency to Cara. Cara was in control of the discussion, and Monica was not pushing anything on her. Instead, Monica was offering a point of view to Cara that she could either accept or decline. Either way, the offering would be received as less threatening because Monica was asking for permission to share, rather than forcing her point of view on Cara. Because of this, Cara reacted in a less defensive way and answered, "Sure. It would be nice to hear an outsider's perspective."

"Great," Monica said, "but I'm not as familiar as you are, so you'll have to let me know if I'm wrong, okay?"

"Sure."

Now that she had permission, Monica could head back to the simple strategy of connecting and collaborating.

"I honestly think," Monica continued, slowing her pace down and facing toward Cara to emphasize her input, "that both of you truly and sincerely care about the school system and want what's best. Do you agree with that statement so far?"

Cara bit her lip in thought, and then nodded. "Yes, I think so."

"So what I'm wondering is, are there any key points on policy that you both agree on?"

"Of course," Cara reflected.

"That's good, so there is some common ground, right?" Monica asked.

"Right."

"Like what?"

"Well, we both think budget cuts are hurting schools," Cara began, "and that the curriculum generally doesn't offer teachers the flexibility they need to really teach anything beyond a superficial level."

"That's great. So do both candidates share those beliefs as well?"

"Not exactly," Cara explained, "Spocard has mentioned her support for increasing the budget but hasn't mentioned anything about focusing on social skills yet."

"And Dirk?"

"I haven't heard him say anything about the budget yet," Cara said, "but he does agree that social skills are an issue."

"It sounds like you and Frank actually have quite a bit in common," Monica observed.

"I guess we do agree on a few things," Cara said, "but I still don't think Dirk is the right one for the job."

"Can I put one more question out there?" Monica asked.

"Sure," Cara answered.

The two of them had made a complete lap around the school, and Cara was clearly back to being herself. Monica had noticed that Cara didn't seem to stress about anything except politics. Her classroom was decorated with all sorts of music posters and pop art, just like Frank's classroom.

"When's the last time you and Frank talked about something other than politics?" Monica asked.

Cara paused for a moment. Her face bent downward into a genuine frown. Monica could see Cara's eyes tracing their way back into a past *before* all of their political disagreements. Monica reflected on her own relationships, how they had felt under assault since the country had taken such an intensely polarized political disposition. She herself longed for the days before cell phones beamed bad news into every conversation and people sneered at the neighbors with whom they disagreed on even one issue. She recalled her life less than a decade ago, when she and her friends would hang out for hours and nothing of great importance would even come up.

"Wow," Cara exhaled, "you know . . . that is a very good question. The truth is, it's been a long time. We used to talk mostly about prog rock, back in the day. You know, like Rush, and Yes, and those kinds of bands."

Monica opened the door back into Serenity Springs High School. The two of them stepped back in and made their way to Cara's classroom.

"I think I understand what you're getting at," Cara told Monica when they arrived at her class, "and I do appreciate it."

"I want to be clear: I'm not trying to get you to not discuss politics anymore or anything like that," Monica said. "I just think sometimes we all need to remember that we're all on the same team."

Cara reentered her classroom and Monica started on her way back. After she had walked for a while, she noticed that there was music coming from Cara's room. It was the first time Monica had heard music from there all year.

*Monica's Journal*

*Tamara Givens on the First Objective*

- *School leaders need to work to pull people together!*

*Emil Harker on Inspiring Others*

- *People will respond well when they feel like they are being a hero.*

- But they won't respond well if they are not being treated like the hero that they are.
- We need to pull them into the process to find the best solutions.
  - Connect and collaborate!

## Dr. Mary Jane Hetrick on Putting Humans First

- Connect as humans first before we seek to understand the issues around the conflict.

# CHAPTER FOURTEEN

# A COOLING EMBER

Diane Flynn was wearing the same hoodie as when Monica had last seen her, and a pair of sweatpants. Her hasty ponytail made another appearance as well. As Monica approached, she realized that the hoodie still had the same coffee stain as before.

Monica had taken a moment to center herself before she approached Diane. She wasn't sure if their last encounter had simply been a bad day for the teacher, or if there was something deeper going on. On their first encounter, Monica had been counting on Diane to build her up.

"Hi Monica." Although Diane didn't sound nearly as grumpy as their previous encounter, she also did not sound cheery. The subtext to her greeting was clear. It said *I'm exhausted.* Again, she was leaning against the wall outside of her class-room. She seemed to be doing her best to smile at the kids as they entered, but Monica could see that even this was a struggle.

"Good to see you this morning, Diane," Monica replied.

"Good to see you too."

"How are you?"

"Fine."

Diane's flat response threatened to suck the air out of the conversation. An awkward silence hung over the two of them for a moment, but Monica was prepared this time. She didn't let her internal monologue shift to wondering if she had done something wrong. She clearly hadn't. Whatever had Diane feeling down clearly had nothing to do with her, and because of that fact, Monica had an opportunity to reach out and connect with her. Maybe Monica could help. Maybe she couldn't. There was only one way to find out.

"Are you facing some rough times?" Monica asked.

"Kind of. I dunno. It's just the job," Diane said.

"Just the job?" Monica prompted.

Diane sighed. "Yeah, you know how it is. Or maybe you don't. Maybe it's different on the admin side. Doesn't matter."

Monica decided to try a more direct approach.

"What is it that's bothering you, Diane? Maybe I can help, but even if I can't, I can at least listen."

"Ha." Diane snorted condescendingly, before catching herself. "Sorry, I don't mean to be rude to you. That's not cool of me. Honestly, the fact is I don't think anyone can really do anything so I should just harden up."

"Alright, here's the deal," Monica said, trying to match Diane's blunt tone. "If you want to come chat or even just vent, I'm happy to listen. Education really is tough, but you're not alone here."

"Thanks," Diane said in a tone that suggested she was writing her off, but then she caught herself a second time. "No, you know what, I think I'll take you up on that. I shouldn't just hold stuff in. The problem is it isn't just one thing. It's a series of realizations I've had about this job over the past several months, maybe years. They ask us to do more and more and we never–"

As if to highlight her point, the bell rang for the class to begin. Diane couldn't help but laugh. Monica saw the humor in the situation and allowed a chuckle to escape.

"Anyway," Diane said, "if you want to talk with me as Monica and not as a counselor, yes, I'm happy to sit down and vent."

"Deal," Monica agreed.

"Thanks for putting it out there," Diane said over her shoulder as she went into her class.

Monica started on her way back down the hall. It had taken some time, and quite a bit of effort, but she was finally connecting with a teacher who was clearly feeling very disconnected from her school. If the school was going to make a cultural shift toward positivity, then teachers like Diane would need to feel engaged and invested. Even more importantly, Monica needed to make sure that all the teachers in the school were taken care of and given recognition for their work.

Teachers are the ultimate key to every school. Teachers made it all work. If a school was negative, Monica knew, that usually meant that the teachers were not being given the support they needed. Monica respected teachers immensely. It was a hard job, and it was an altruistic job. She saw teachers as the keepers of the torch of hope.

Monica wasn't sure what it was that had Diane so deflated, but she knew that both she and the school needed to do everything within their power to get all their teachers feeling happy, confident, supported, and appreciated in their school.

But at the same time, Diane clearly wasn't ready to open up just yet. Monica recognized her own limits in this situation. She accepted that Diane had the freedom to open up or not, and that either way Monica was going to do the best she could with whatever reality put in front of her. Monica let out a deep sigh, allowing herself to relax into the truth of her situation. Recognizing that truth was calming. There was no need for her to carry anxiety just because things weren't in her control. She would influence what she could and trust that the rest would sort itself out.

## Monica's Journal

### Adam Lustig on Supporting Staff

- Make sure we are focusing on the social-emotional wellness of our staff.
  - What type of supports are we providing?
- Make sure we are bringing the disengaged individual to the table, so they have a voice and are involved.

- Recognize that teaching is a grind, so celebrate and recognize teachers' work!
- Keep building community and relationships at the core of your work.

## Tamara Givens on Supporting Staff

- Help the teacher find something else on campus that they can contribute to, what they care about doing on campus, and support them in those things.
- Usually it is not the kids that cause burnout; it is other adults who burn the teachers out.
  - Work with teachers to foster friendly relationships on campus.
  - Help teachers find what they are passionate about on campus.

# CHAPTER FIFTEEN

# TRADING VINEGAR FOR HONEY

Dale was pacing back and forth in his apartment. Not even Patches could distract him from his current train of thought.

GOLFMAST3R_DAD3288 had been trying to convince the parents to sign a petition to prevent the fundraiser from being organized next semester, and if he succeeded, that meant that the school was not going to have the new supplies the staff was hoping for. When he spoke with Monica, she had suggested that Mr. Dale ask GOLFMAST3R_DAD3288 to come in and speak with him in person and gave him an outline on how to have a conversation with him.

Dale looked at his screen. The last message he had sent to GOLFMAST3R_DAD3288 hadn't yet received a response.

MrDale42: I was wondering if we could meet up in person to talk about some of your ideas. I see how important it is to you that we get this right, so I want to invite you to help us make the best choice.

The lack of response spoke volumes. Already Monica's ideas were working.

Dale looked at the notes he had taken.

- Who is this, anyway? You should find out who you're talking to.

It was silly that he didn't even know which parent this was. It was an embarrassing oversight for Dale. He simply hadn't taken the time to ask, since he had gotten defensive pretty quickly. Fortunately, Monica had seemed to understand and told him, "I totally understand. It's hard when discussions are intense."

Dale had learned later that the person behind the screen name was Harvey Higgs, and that his daughter was one of Dale's students.

Dale's eyes traced farther down on the page.

- First acknowledge his value.
  - Skeptical
  - Critical thinker
  - *Speaks his mind*
- Second, ask for his help.

Dale had asked Monica what to do if GOLFMAST3R_ DAD3288 said he didn't want to help.

"Would I be off the hook then?" Dale had asked.

Monica had answered, "Ha, well . . . maybe. But we want to be sure, right? So I think what I'd do is gently insist. Try to put him in the role of the hero. He clearly wants to be acknowledged, just like all of us, so why not give that to him? It's no sweat for you to tell him you'd really like his help."

- Third, present the situation to him and ask for solutions.
  - Who knows? Maybe he'll come up with a way to raise a whole bunch of money for the school.
  - Alternatively, if he can't, then you can put him on the track to look, which will give him a goal that could be helpful.

Dale was beginning to understand what Monica was getting at when she had explained the best way to defeat an enemy was to make them an ally. As he was contemplating this, a response popped up.

```
GOLFMAST3R_DAD3288:  You mean for the
    scam?
```

This was Dale's chance. All he needed to do was keep his cool and stick to the script. He resisted the urge to respond defensively, he knew having parents involved in the school culture was actually a good thing. So, he took a deep breath, and felt the emotion flare up in himself. After a few moments, it passed, and he was able to react with a much clearer mind.

```
MrDale42: See,   that's   the   thing.
    It's  clear  that  you're  willing
    to  speak  your  mind,  and  you  think
    critically,  so  I  think  the  school
    could  really  benefit  from  hearing
    what  you  have  to  say.  I  think  it
    would  be  good  to  get  your  opinion
    on  all  the  info  we  have.
GOLFMAST3R_DAD3288:  I  dunno,  man.
    I'm  pretty  busy.
```

MrDale42: I totally get that, but
    here's the thing. Most people
    just kind of go with the flow. You
    speak your mind, and that's what
    we really need, Harvey. People
    who speak their mind are rare.
    I honestly think you could really
    help the school.
GOLFMAST3R_DAD3288: Yeah,okay,sure.
    I guess I can help.

"It worked!" Dale clapped his hands together once in excitement and pushed himself back from his computer. Patches, startled, scrambled off the desk at the sudden outburst.

"That's unreal!" Dale said to himself. "Holy smokes . . . I feel like I just unlocked a superpower. That's some Jedi-level skills right there."

GOLFMAST3R_DAD3288: I can meet
    Thursday after school.
MrDale42: Perfect. Thank you for
    offering up your time to help the
    school.

Dale stood up and walked around the room for a moment before deciding to head out for a walk. He threw on his jacket and hat and shuffled out the door.

He was still surprised at how smoothly it had all gone. Monica had seemed pretty confident, whereas Dale had been a little skeptical, but open to the possibility that it could work. He certainly didn't expect the exchange to go that well. It seemed almost unbelievable. This guy had been the bane of Dale's existence for months, and now he had an opportunity to redirect him in a way that might even benefit the school.

The idea of a helpful Harvey felt like a long shot, but at the very least he'd probably come to realize that the fundraiser was actually about as good as it gets. It was a win either way for the school.

Fall offered a comfortable nostalgia to Dale. There was something about bundling up just a little with a hoodie, a warm hat, and a light jacket that felt comfy to him. It reminded him of his own time in high school. He and his friends had participated in fundraisers not much different from the one they had coming up. Sure, theirs was more digital in nature, but that gave the kids a much greater reach than he had back then. Back in his time, he and his friends had gone door to door on their bicycles trying to raise money for their school.

Dale struggled to remember what prize had so strongly incentivized him that fall of his first year.

He hopped over one of the many puddles that dotted the sidewalk.

*A soccer net!* Dale suddenly recalled. *It was a soccer net!*

He smiled to himself, remembering how he and his friends had gotten just enough to pool their donations together for that soccer net. He chuckled to himself as he recalled the beating they gave that thing. It had withstood the chaos of his friend group for years. It survived the whole crew's best attempts at destruction: blasting shots, hitting the post, and even running into it over and over again until the summer between his freshman and sophomore year of college when a particularly nasty storm finally damaged it beyond repair.

"Good times," he caught himself mumbling to himself out loud.

The thought that some of the kids he was teaching now might be able to enjoy some version of that filled him with hope and determination, as he swung the door to the local cafe open and stepped in for a victory latte.

# COLLABORATION

# CHAPTER SIXTEEN

# ONE PROBLEM TOO MANY

After dropping Mike off at the airport, Monica returned to her empty house. She let out a big sigh. It was a stressful time for both of them. Monica was busy trying to transform her school's culture and Mike was flying off to train a brand-new branch.

She was used to having Mike by her side. They did so well as a team. But for the next two weeks, she would be taking on life independently. She did enjoy her own company and knew that she would have a good time by herself for a while, but the disruption from normality still came at a time when she would have much rather remained in her comfortable routine.

Mike had taken an early flight, and Monica had an extra 30 minutes to herself. She spent that time making herself a cup of green tea, some toast, and one egg over easy.

She took inventory of her emotions as she ate. She knew she had a lot of work ahead of her. She felt the pressure of the school's needs. She knew she would need to push for a while before the positive effects of school culture really took hold. However, despite all that effort she knew was in her immediate future, she felt calm. Monica knew that all of the tasks that remained to be done were within her ability to do; she was confident in her ability to handle all the situations at hand.

Over the years, Monica had garnered greater self-efficacy by persevering through failures. Resilience, perseverance, self-efficacy–they were all related. They were all skills that could be grown and developed. Five years ago, she would have been stressed out by Mike being gone during such a busy time. She had come a long way since then. She could handle the problems the school faced. She knew it.

Monica stepped outside. The morning promised a warm and pleasant day, perhaps the last one for the season as fall was in full swing, and as Monica got into her car and put her key in the ignition, she thought to herself, *I can handle this.*

She turned the key. The engine did not respond at all.

She tried a second time, and again, there was no response.

Anxiety began to set in. Monica was instantly knocked off her emotional center by the failure of the car to start. If the car had just started, she could have certainly made it into school early, got a jump on the day, and even gotten a lead on her week. But this was just one thing more than she wanted to handle. She was already at her maximum capacity, and this felt like the straw that broke the camel's back.

Panic began to set in. Monica tried to fight it, but everything suddenly felt like it was falling apart. Suddenly, the endless task list at school, the countless social-emotional problems, the absence of her husband, the conflicts surrounding the teachers and students, and the car troubles all glared down at her at once. Every little issue compounded into one giant monster. Even the weather seemed to turn in that instant, with the wind picking up unexpectedly. Monica tried turning the key a third time, but the monster of anxiety and negativity saw to it that her efforts were met with an unyielding silence from her car. Monica's world was crumbling around her.

She closed her eyes and fought for her own cognitive control but her inner monologue was already ranting: *Of course something like this would happen today. Just when I most need everything to go okay to keep my head above water, this car won't start, so now I'll be late, and I'll be behind, and all day I'll be struggling to play catch up, and I'll bet there's going to be something else that pops up because something always does, and of course there's only going to be more and more work today and then later today when I get home I'll need to cook dinner or something even though tonight is usually Mike's night to cook so there goes another half hour at least that I'll fall behind, and who knows how much it's going to cost to fix this car! Wait a minute. Wait. Pull it back. Get it back under control. Breathe. Yeah, just breathe.*

Monica decided to do a few breathing squares. Dale had mentioned them in their meeting a few weeks ago, and it had reminded her of how useful they could be in high-anxiety moments. She took in a deep breath and held it for a count of four seconds. Then she exhaled for four seconds. Then she held the breath out for four more seconds before finally drawing in her next four-second breath.

In for four. Hold for four. Out for four. Hold for four. Repeat.

After her fifth breathing square she was ready to step back into her present situation again.

*Okay,* she thought to herself, *one thing at a time. Let's try the battery charger.*

Monica popped her trunk, grabbed her battery charger from under her seat, and attached it to her car's battery. After she had carefully followed all of its instructions, she tried to start her car again. Again, she got nothing. *I know I have gas, so it can't be that. Maybe it's the ignition? How would I check? If the battery is good, but the ignition is bad, my headlights will turn on even though the car won't start.*

Monica turned on her headlights. They switched on without any issue.

*Okay, so it might be ignition. If so, that's only a few hundred bucks or so. That's not fun, but it could be worse. I can call my mobile mechanic, Billy, to see if he can handle it while I'm at work today, so my next priority will be to get a ride to school. Who lives nearby?*

Monica considered her options. Fortunately, it was early, and Principal Hannah Shore probably hadn't left yet. Hannah was reasonably close by and could probably pick her up.

Monica called Principal Shore and asked for a ride.

"Of course!" Hannah said. "I could use the company. See you in a few minutes."

Having addressed that issue, Monica continued down her checklist, calling Billy and asking him if he could come check on the car later that afternoon.

"Oh sure," Billy said sleepily, "I have an opening at around 2:00 p.m. I'll swing on by. Can you leave the keys somewhere so I can work on it then?"

Monica agreed and hid her keys for Billy to find. *Okay, so . . . now what remains?*

Nothing else remained.

In less than 10 minutes, the crisis that had seemed impossible to overcome had dissolved due to her simple, step-by-step actions. The monster that had seemed so overwhelming had already been defanged, and she was left once again with no more than the tasks of her school day.

*And as far as dinner goes*, she thought to herself, *I'm just going to order Chinese food, so I can check that worry off too!*

Just like that, Monica was back to baseline.

Self-efficacy doesn't mean everything will go right. In fact, it's guaranteed that something will go wrong at some point more or less every day. But having self-efficacy means you don't have to worry about those problems because when they arise, you can and will handle them.

Just then, Monica got a text from Mike. It read:

About to board, thanks for the ride again—all good with you too? ♥

As Hannah was pulling into her driveway to pick her up, Monica texted back:

All good here too. Have a safe flight! ♥

Monica hopped into Hannah's car and was greeted cheerfully by her friend and co-worker. There would be struggles today, and tomorrow, and the day after that. And they would all be resolved, just like the countless challenges she and her community had handled before.

*Monica's Journal*

*Tamara Givens on High-Stress Moments*

- *Life is a journey, not a destination.*
- *We can get through everything eventually.*
- *Just break it down to smaller steps . . . brick by brick.*

# CHAPTER SEVENTEEN

# FREEDOM THROUGH ACCEPTANCE

The week flew by. Monica managed to handle her car troubles, but the majority of her time after that had been dedicated to paperwork. She was tired of her office and wanted to spend some time outside. She had also noticed Hannah was under greater stress than usual, and so she'd invited Hannah to a walking meeting. Hannah had gratefully accepted.

"I've thought quite a bit about what you said," Hannah told Monica as they walked around the perimeter of the school.

It was the Thursday before Halloween weekend, and the majority of the leaves had fallen from the trees, so each step they took made a satisfying crunch. It was early in the afternoon, and there was a calm, cool, relaxed atmosphere hanging across campus. Time itself seemed to relax from its hurried shuffle into a leisurely stroll.

"You know, about accepting the reality of my situation as principal," Hannah continued, "and I've arrived at the conclusion that this job has changed so much that my previous objectives and goals are just no longer reasonable."

"I agree," Monica said. "That kind of gives you a new freedom to define the role, doesn't it?"

"Exactly!" Hannah said, "It's wild. When you first explained the idea of examining reality as it is and accepting it, I was worried it would feel like a prison. But now I realize, it's the only way to find any real freedom. So, for example, my idea of being able to keep every parent happy all the time? Nope. Not possible. Not in this reality. I can address some things, but not all. So what's my new goal, with my new reality? I'm going to focus on the big stuff first and designate a time for the parents to reach out . . . except for emergencies, of course."

"Of course," Monica agreed, glad to be back on the social side of her occupation.

There were groups of students scattered across the field. One group of kids played frisbee in their PE class. Another group sat on a giant quilt, chatting away for their free study hour. A third group formed a circle, kicking a hacky sack among themselves.

"But it hasn't been easy. In fact," Hannah explained, "I haven't been particularly successful in this new approach because I'm still trying to create those boundaries for myself. There's just so much criticism coming my way all the time, so I was wondering if you wouldn't mind explaining how it is that you handle that sort of thing? I've seen the results since you've joined the team; what's your method?"

"Sure, I'm happy to help," Monica replied. "Let's see how well I can articulate this. The first thing to know is that when conflict sets in, like when we get criticized or challenged, our own emotions are a factor we need to acknowledge and manage. The reality of the situation is that we are probably going to feel at least a little emotional–maybe even a lot–and so we want to keep a really simple model in our head that helps to steer the conversation in a positive way. It's hard to be sophisticated when we're emotionally activated, you know? So we need to keep it simple. I usually try to think of it in two steps: connect and collaborate."

"That makes sense to me," Hannah said. "I always think if we can start from a place where we're on the same side, the same team, that we can find mutual success. But sometimes it's hard to see common ground, especially when someone is criticizing me and being combative."

"Oh, for sure. It's not easy. But if you can find just one little piece of truth that you can agree with, then you're in," Monica explained. "We can workshop that a bit, if you'd like."

"Yes, that would be really helpful. Okay, let's get specific. I've got this parent who is so upset that her kid didn't get the math teacher they wanted this year. And she said, 'When are you finally going to get organized?' What would you say to that?"

"Hijack the impulse to become defensive," Monica said, "and that comes back to the feeling navigation part. When our ego or status is under attack, we get defensive because we're worried our status will decline. But by dropping that and letting vulnerability come through, we can avoid the ego trap. So I'd say something like, 'It hurts to hear you ask that,' which instantly puts you in a position where you're being honest, and her in a position where she hasn't been attacked, because all you're saying is how you feel. Then I'd flip the script immediately with, 'but if I put myself in your shoes . . .' and then find that point of truth where you can meet them."

"Got it. So now we've taken away the chance to be defensive and started the connection process by connecting with them. I'm essentially defending their behavior for them so they don't have to," Hannah noted.

"Exactly," Monica said.

"Okay, and then what?" Hannah asked, excitedly. Monica could tell this was a situation that had troubled Hannah, and she actively wanted to resolve it.

"Then you check in to make sure you're on the same page," Monica said. "Nothing complicated, just something like, 'Is that right?' or 'Am I on the right track?' so that they have a chance to clarify, because then you'll know for certain that you are, in fact, on the same page."

"Okay, I think I've got it. We give them the benefit of the doubt, but then make sure that what we're pointing to is actually true," Hannah noted.

"Correct," Monica confirmed, "and if they say 'yes,' then we can start to look for a common solution, or create an expectation or boundary based on the reality of the situation."

"Okay, let me try," Hannah said. "In the instance of the parent I was talking about earlier, I might say something like, 'I recognize that your son wants to be in Mr. Garcia's math class, and I get it, he's a great teacher, but with the electives your son has, we simply can't make it work because the schedules don't match at any point. But let's try to turn our sights on next semester and see what we can do.' Would that work?"

"It might," Monica said. "But even if it doesn't, you've passed the ball to them. So regardless of what their answer is, you're trying to make it work, and trying to collaborate with them for a solution."

"I know if I could have gotten them to that point, we could have started down that road," Hannah said, "but I couldn't get them to stop being combative."

"Keep in mind," Monica noted, "that if they're just too combative, you can always put the conversation on hold by saying something like, 'I don't think this conversation is serving either of us right now; let's pick up this discussion at a later time.' You don't need to take abuse."

"Boundaries," Hannah said.

"Boundaries," Monica agreed.

They had made a full lap around the school and had almost returned to the office. Monica was glad for the chance to stretch her legs with Hannah.

"One more question," Hannah said, "how would you handle it if you just straight-up disagree with them?"

"Similar idea: first you reduce the potential for someone to feel defensive. I like to do that by giving them the opportunity to ask my opinion. Something like, 'That's interesting, I'm wondering why you think . . .' whatever it is they're thinking."

"And if they don't ask your opinion?"

"Then," Monica advised, "you offer the hook a little more directly. Maybe something like, 'I guess I see things differently,' and if they don't go for it then, I might even just ask directly, 'Are you open to a different perspective?' That way you're never threatening them and hearing your point of view is something they have agreed to. Then just present your idea and see if there's part of it that they agree with. Does that make sense?"

"Yeah, I think so. Not asking them to agree completely, just seeing if there's any common ground," Hannah said.

"Exactly."

"Thank you, Monica, this was a great idea," Hannah said as they approached their cars. "I really appreciate you getting me away from my desk for a bit."

"You're welcome," Monica said, "maybe we can have more walk-and-talk meetings in the future."

"Deal," Hannah replied.

## Monica's Journal

### Dr. Stephanie Eberts on Burnout

- A lot of our educators and educational leaders are feeling burnt out.
  - The solution is for them to continue to educate because that is what they are good at.
  - So they have to take it upon themselves to educate the community.
    - Helping other people to understand what teachers do on a day-to-day basis.
    - Discussing how parents can participate, and how people can become part of the school culture.

### Emil Harker on Rewiring Conflict

- We need to rewire our idea of conflict and respond in a different way.

- This is resolved by hijacking the impulsive desire to become defensive.
  - We can do this in four easy steps:
    1. Sharing our feelings and reasons in a vulnerable way.
    2. Using a transition statement such as, "but if I see it from your point of view" or "if I look at it from your angle."
    3. Then stating what you think it is like to be in the other person's shoes.
    4. Finally, checking in to see if you are right in stating how the person feels.

# CHAPTER EIGHTEEN

# BREAKTHROUGH

The week after Halloween, Tony sat in Monica's office with his arms crossed, staring to the right side of the room, avoiding eye contact with Monica. In fact, he didn't even acknowledge that she was in the room at all. He wore a dark gray hoodie, which he had pulled up upon arriving in the office, and jeans that were worn through on the knees. He reminded Monica of the skateboarders at her school from back when she was a kid.

*Wow, it's funny how things come back into style*, she thought to herself, but knew better than to point it out to him.

"How are we doing today, Tony?" Monica asked, trying to hold a tone that was both neutral and inviting at the same time.

"Ms. Betty already told me," Tony said.

"What did she tell you?"

Tony glanced at Monica, but then broke eye contact again. "She said if I keep screwing up, you're sending me off to be with other rejects."

Tony's negativity was surprising to Monica. Betty had reported that Tony had been more receptive to her since Monica had started coaching her, and that they had connected pretty well. She was more optimistic than she had been in a while, and after a week of using the code word and connecting, she was beginning to think he could turn it around. Monica knew that Tony was learning to trust Betty, but that he didn't trust Monica—at least not yet.

"Well, hold on," Monica said, "that's not why you're here. And I don't think of you as a reject."

"Isn't that what this is for?" Tony said. "I'm not dumb. I wouldn't be here if I wasn't in trouble. You can try to sound nice, but it's just your job, and you don't actually care. Everything's just an assembly line. I don't fit in, so it's either learn to fit in or get thrown in the trash with all the other defective products."

Monica realized this was going to be harder than she had imagined. Even before any conversation had begun, Tony was feeling defensive. The meeting hadn't been a surprise to him, and Betty had discussed the idea of Tony meeting with Monica with him when she had first set out to connect and collaborate with him. This was not a surprise; it had been scheduled and explained as a check-in to see how he was, but Tony seemed to see it as a confrontation. Monica took a calm breath in and let the emotions she felt run their course. She did not ignore them, and instead she directed them to the goal of mutual understanding.

"You're not a product, you're a person," Monica said.

She let the silence sit. Tony glanced up at her, then back down again. He shifted in his seat uncomfortably. His face had shifted slightly. Now he was showing pain, rather than hostility.

"Listen," Monica said. "You want me to be honest with you, right?"

"Yeah."

"Okay, then let's start there," Monica said. "I'm going to be honest and direct with you. I'm not going to try to lie or make things seem better than they are. If you think I'm being dishonest, or if I'm just flat out wrong, you can call me out. In return, I'm going to assume the same honesty from you. Deal?"

Tony considered the offer for a moment. Then he looked up at Monica and said, "Okay. Deal."

"Alright." Monica took a deep breath. "You're right. Part of my job is to try to keep the social side of the school running smoothly. That's true. But there are two things I think we can establish right away. One, I absolutely do not see you as a product. You are a person. I care about you as a person, even if the system doesn't. And I get it Tony, I really do, the system *does* suck. It absolutely sucks and I am intimately familiar with that fact. Do you believe me when I say that?"

"I dunno. I guess we'll see."

"Fair enough," Monica agreed, "the other thing is this: a product can't think, and a product can't make decisions, but you can. Do we agree there?"

"I don't know if free will exists," Tony said.

"Honestly, I don't know if it does either, but we know at least that a product doesn't have it. A product doesn't have free will, but you might. Fair?"

"Fair. I might. I'm not saying I do for sure, but I might."

Tony was clearly a deep thinker. Much of the reason he hated school was because he was often bored. While other students were focused on the core curriculum, he was more interested in big, strange ideas that aren't typically taught until undergraduate philosophy.

"It's hard to go through this system," Monica said, "and I know sometimes you just want to give a big middle finger to the whole thing, and honestly I don't blame you."

"But?" Tony assumed.

"There's no 'but,'" Monica said. "I'm just letting you know that I get it. The system is not perfect. Some of us are trying to make it better, but we're still figuring out how, and struggling every day. All I know to do is to try to take every person and every moment one at a time. So there is no 'but' or anything like that. It's hard, and that's the reality of the situation. So given that reality, we can either accept it, work with what we've got, and make the best of it, or we can sweep it under the rug and it'll probably get worse. If we do indeed have free will, that's the choice we're going to need to make. I can't tell you what to do. All I can tell you is that facing reality and working with it *will absolutely* make things a little better. And from what Ms. Betty has told me, you've been doing a great job of communicating with her this week."

Tony uncrossed his arms and leaned forward on the couch; he put his head in his hands and took a deep breath. This wasn't a bad kid. This was a kid in pain. This was someone who was hurting and who needed someone else to just understand what he was going through.

"You don't have to tell me anything," Monica said, "but if you want to, you can. Maybe I can help, I don't know, but I absolutely will listen."

"I don't want to . . ." Tony's voice trailed off, muffled in his hands.

"I'm sorry, I didn't hear that?"

Tony looked up at Monica, "I don't want to go away to a different school."

"Then don't," Monica said. "If you don't want to go to a different school, then make the choice to engage in this one. We have a place for you here, if you just decide to join us. Your teachers, the administrators, me—we're not your enemies, Tony. We're just people. And we're all rooting for you. We *like* you."

"Why? Why would you like me when I come in and wreck your—I dunno—system? Whatever this is, I'm always screwing it up."

"Because we all feel exactly the way you feel, sometimes," Monica said, "Believe me, we felt it when we were your age, and we feel it as adults now. The only difference is that we've made a decision you haven't made yet, and that isn't your fault. It's a decision that takes time and you don't need to rush it."

"And what decision is that?" Tony asked.

"To look at the system, to see that it's flawed, and to be good to the people in our lives anyway. Like I said, the system has serious flaws, and clearly we are both aware of them. Our choice is to either give up or make the best of our situation. The fact of the matter is, and I say this based on both empirical data *and* first-hand experience, if we try to improve things, they do indeed improve. But that starts with a choice. That choice is to try to help yourself and then to help other people, not because you think you'll make more money, or get recognition, fame, or anything like that, but because it's just the right thing to do," said Monica.

"There are many ways of making that happen," she continued, "and what I see in you is the ability to see problems clearly. We need more of that. Other people don't necessarily see the things you see, even when you point it out to them. We don't just *like* you, Tony. We *need* you. As a society, we need you and people like you to join us in trying to make things better. I know it's easy to get angry and to shut yourself away, but what good will that do? What if, instead, you took that ability and you hopped into our student leader-ship program?"

"What difference can that make?" Tony asked.

"I don't know. Could it make things 1% better? If so, isn't that worth it? Imagine if all of us decided to do something every day to make life 1% better, wouldn't that be enough to change the world?"

"I guess so," Tony said, "but it would take a long-ass time."

"Yes," Monica agreed, "you're right. It's going to take a long time, and a lot of work. And that is the choice, Tony. It's a difficult choice, but every night I sleep like a baby because my conscience is clear. It's clear because I know that every once in a while I get to talk to somebody like you who has the capacity to be good, and who has the potential to make this world so much better, and if I can work with you to make your life good enough, then maybe you can get a chance to make that potential real."

Tears were forming in Tony's eyes.

"So that's the real reason you're in my office today, Tony," Monica said. "You're here because I want to help make your life a little better if I can. You're not here because of a system, or a protocol, or some social machine that wants you to fall in line. You're here because there are people in this building that have made the decision to play as a team, and we'd really like for you to join us. We like you, and we want you to be happy, and we want you on our team."

Tony sat in silence, considering Monica's words.

From Monica's point of view, all she had done was tell him the truth of her own beliefs. Indeed, what she said *was* what she believed. She understood that connection can only occur in the light of honesty, and that she had no reason to try to be deceptive. Therefore she spoke as clearly and truthfully as she could, all the while giving the troubled young man the benefit of the doubt.

"I get what you're saying," Tony said. "We learned in math class how compounding works. I know that if everyone did just a little bit of good every day, we could probably fix things. I just feel like I'm in a cage sometimes, you know?"

"I know," Monica said, "but remember, if free will does exist, you always have a choice. That's what freedom is: facing reality and deciding what you're going to do."

"But how could it actually even matter?" Tony pushed back. "I've been drowning in meaninglessness for so long."

"That's one of the toughest questions we can face, and I can't really give you an answer to that. But I can tell you my own experience," Monica continued, speaking the next statement very slowly and clearly. "My own life began to feel meaningful when I started to help other people."

Tony nodded and sat quietly for a moment before asking, "So . . . what do we do now?"

"All I want to do today is to check in on you and see if we can help, Tony," Monica said. "That's literally my entire agenda right now. Here, look, you can see my notes."

*Monica's Journal*

**To Do for Today**
- *Meeting with Tony.*
  - *Are things okay?*
  - *How can we help?*
  - *What interests does he have?*
  - *Can the school meet those interests?*

Tony reviewed the notes. "I guess . . . I don't know. I don't think I'm okay."

"Do you want to talk about it?" Monica asked.

"I dunno. Yes? I guess. just . . . " Tony struggled to communicate his feelings. "Things are hard at home. I dunno. Life is hard."

"Life is hard," Monica agreed.

"I don't think I want to talk about it right now, actually," Tony realized.

"That's okay. We don't have to. But even without having that conversation, is there anything we can do to help?"

"I'm just so sad and angry all the time," Tony said, his voice rising slightly. "It's like, I just can't even remember the last time something good happened. It's like, every time you look online it's bad things happening everywhere, all the time, and innocent people just getting wrecked by natural disasters and governments doing all sorts of horrible things. How can anyone *live like this?*"

"What is happening right now?" Monica asked.

"There's a war that's . . . " Tony started.

"No, I mean in terms of your own experience. Right now. Here, in this room. Is anything bad happening?"

"Well . . . no, I guess not really," Tony said.

"And do you have any control over the things that are happening outside of this room, in this moment?" Monica asked.

"No."

"And are any of those things your fault?"

"I guess not."

"Then you aren't responsible for them right now," Monica explained. "The only thing you're responsible for right now is for yourself and what you need. So Tony, what do you need?"

"That's the worst part. I kind of just . . . don't know," Tony realized, "I really don't know."

Monica took the statement in for a moment and then said, "One of the tough things in life is that it's sometimes hard to even know what we need for ourselves. Would you be open to a suggestion from me?"

"Yes," Tony said.

"I think you need a chance to hang out with friends your age who also share your enthusiasm for thinking critically,"

Monica said, "and there are a few ways to do that. Off the top of my head, I think you'd like debate, or I could see you being a contributor to the student leadership program we have here, or maybe you can focus those feelings into something physical like wrestling. Those are just the first that come to mind."

Tony evaluated those groups for a moment. He seemed tentatively interested.

"I think I'd be willing to try something like debate," Tony said, "but I'm not sure."

"How about you give it a try, no pressure. If you like it you can go for it; if not, then no obligation," Monica suggested.

"Yeah . . . I mean, I wouldn't be doing anything better so, I guess why not."

Tony was clearly in need of something to challenge and engage him. Monica knew that it might take some time to find that fit, but it seemed that at the very least he was willing to try. As the two of them made plans for Tony to begin debate, Monica felt a wave of gratitude toward Betty. She could have given up on him. It would have been reasonable and appropriate to want to dismiss him to a different class, but instead she stuck with him.

Monica and Tony agreed to have a check-in every once in a while. Tony seemed to like the idea. Monica knew that not every student would react so favorably, but it looked like this one in particular might end up doing just fine. There was no denying, he had some problems he needed to work on, but truth be told Monica had been that way too when she was younger. Most of the teachers she knew had experienced similar questions and feelings. There was a sort of secret legacy of rebels who sorted themselves out and went on to help other little rebels to sort themselves out in turn. It was a very cool legacy to be a part of.

### Monica's Journal

### Dr. Stephanie Eberts on Dealing with Difficult Students

- Ask the teacher to find ways to build a true relationship with the difficult student.
  - Have conversations with them.
  - Provide positive labeling with regard to who they are.
  - Give them some responsibility in the classroom.

# CHAPTER NINETEEN

# FACE TO FACE

The Internet feuders, Sandra and Maya, sat in Monica's office. Monica could see that both of them were clearly uncomfortable. Neither of them looked at each other, choosing instead to examine the floor. The halls were still buzzing with the movement of students from one period to the next, but after a few minutes, the sound faded away. Instantly, the halls became empty, and the silence left the two of them feeling even more uncomfortable.

There was no denying it, the situation was tense. Neither of the girls had spoken with each other in a very long time, and neither of them felt inclined to start. Both of them shared a challenging nausea in their stomach that heralded the uncomfortable exchange they both knew would come next.

Monica had coached Maya on how to handle the situation, and Maya had said she was ready, but Monica knew that this was not an easy situation for anyone to handle.

Even to someone who had no awareness of the situation, it would have been clear that the scene was tense. There was clearly an unresolved conflict that both of the girls were aware of, but neither wanted to bring up. Monica knew this would be a difficult moment for both of them. She had taken the time to clear her mind and relax before this meeting so that she could be centered and present. She took a smooth, steady breath, just as much for herself as for her role as the calm, cool, counselor.

Monica knew that the most important, long-term objective was to implement a program that prevented these sorts of online conflicts, and that the program would need students to teach their peers how to avoid such mistakes. This was an opportunity to teach these two young people how to address conflicts. They could, through this experience, learn skills that would serve them not just now, but throughout the rest of their lives. Maybe then, if directed carefully, they could guide others as well.

But the most recent post from Sandra was even more aggressive than the last. It read:

    Better watch your back, traitor.

Sandra clearly knew that she had crossed a line that she shouldn't have, but this wasn't about punishment. This was about resolving a conflict in a way that served everyone involved.

"Sandra, I believe Maya has something she'd like to tell you," Monica prompted.

Maya sat up straight and took a deep breath.

"Sandra, we've been friends for a long time, and I really value our friendship. So it really hurt me to see the posts that you made about me."

A good start, she had clearly expressed how she felt. Next she would need to relate so that Sandra would connect rather than feel defensive.

Maya continued, "But I think, if I were in your shoes and I thought that I had betrayed your trust, then I would be angry, too."

Monica had only given her that much of a script to start from. Other than that, she told her to be honest and give Sandra the benefit of the doubt. She had remembered the script perfectly and had used it to position the conversation in a way that had a good chance at leading to a positive outcome.

Maya's expression became much more emotional as she departed from her rehearsed opening, into her authentic feelings, "But that's not even how it was! Norbert came up to me and started talking to me about stuff, and it's like, just because you think he's cute doesn't mean I can't talk with him. I wasn't trying to betray you, I was just making a new friend, and it's like, I just hate this! It's so stupid and he's just a boy, and I'm not trying to be a bad friend or anything, but it's like he likes me so what am I even supposed to do?"

"Maya, I'm so sorry!" Sandra exclaimed, "I don't even know why I was posting all those mean things! At first, I felt hurt but then it wasn't even about that, and I don't know why I kept making posts and I feel like it all just got so stupid, and mean, and out of hand. Please don't hate me."

"I don't hate you." Maya's voice was shaking. "I just don't want to fight, and I don't want you to hate me."

"I don't! I just want to be friends again and have it be like before all of this dumb stuff," Sandra said.

"It sounds to me like both of you want to be friends, and want each other to be okay," Monica observed. "Is that right?"

They both agreed.

Sandra leaned over from her chair and reached her hands out to Maya. Maya reciprocated with a hug. The two friends held each other for a moment.

"So what happened here, ladies?" Monica asked, once they had returned to their seats.

"I think . . . I didn't talk to Maya when I should have," Sandra said. "If I had just talked to her in person then maybe none of this would have even started."

"I think that's right," Monica agreed. "It sounds to me like most of this conflict took place online. Isn't this the first time you've spoken in person since all of this started?"

"Yes," Sandra said.

"So . . . what can we do in the future to make sure something like this doesn't happen again?" Monica asked.

The girls thought for a moment, and then Sandra said, "I think maybe these talks shouldn't happen online."

"Yeah," Maya agreed, "we should just settle things in person—and not make assumptions!"

"Good observations," Monica said.

From the initial point of connection, which Maya had established very well, the two of them soon relaxed back into their friendship. They even joked around together a bit about how silly it was that they had gotten upset about something so trivial.

Monica asked the two of them if they had any interest in helping others to avoid problems like theirs. She explained that they wouldn't have to go into specifics, but that they could teach the methods they had learned to other students.

Maya was interested and agreed to help out. Monica added her name to the list of student leaders who could lead her peer-to-peer program.

"Thank you for having this conversation, ladies," Monica said. "Maya, you can go, but Sandra, I want to talk a little longer with you if that's okay. No discipline or anything like that! I just want to chat."

After Maya had left, Monica turned to Sandra and asked, "How are you doing, Sandra? I know that was not an easy conversation."

"It was okay. In my head, I kept thinking it would be way worse."

"Yeah," Monica understood that truth very well. "That's usually how conflicts go. It always seems like it's going to be this big thing. Sometimes it is, but usually it's not nearly as big of a deal as we imagine it to be. And most people are very understanding."

Monica had looked into Sandra's records. She was a good student, but she didn't have any extracurricular activities at all throughout her three years at Serenity Springs High School. Monica wondered if maybe her acting out on social media was a cry for help from someone who was feeling isolated.

"But what about in everyday life? Are you doing okay?" Monica asked.

"Well . . . I don't know." Sandra hesitated.

Monica waited, listening patiently, trying very hard to hear everything that Sandra was saying, and making sure to provide relaxed space for her to finish her thought.

Sandra thought for a moment before admitting, "I don't really have many friends. I feel kind of cut off, I guess."

"That must be tough."

"It is! I mean . . . I don't want to make excuses, but . . . I kind of think that the reason I was making all those comments was because I was getting a bunch of likes. That's kind of messed up, I guess, but I think that's why I was doing it."

Monica was impressed with how quickly Sandra had identified the cause of her behavior. It was clear that she had spent time doing some self-reflecting.

"Sandra, I'm wondering," Monica asked, "what kind of hobbies do you have? What do you like to do?"

Sandra seemed sheepish, answering, "I don't really do much of anything. I don't really like to be the center of attention."

Monica noted the challenge Sandra faced. She wanted to be part of a community, and wanted connection, but didn't feel comfortable having people focusing on her. It made sense that she would use social media to connect, but Monica wondered if there weren't better options.

"I understand that feeling," Monica said. "The spotlight isn't exactly my thing either."

Monica's own words inspired an idea, but she didn't want to push anything on Sandra.

"Would you be interested in hearing a suggestion? No pressure, just an idea?" Monica asked.

"Sure," Sandra said.

"I wonder—how would you feel about working backstage? I mean that literally. The theater program always needs people to work backstage, and I just get the feeling you'd be really good at it."

Sandra considered the idea. She imagined herself high up on the catwalk, directing lights down on stage. She could participate in the show without anyone seeing her. She thought of hanging out with the theater kids but not having to stand up and say lines. She imagined herself setting up scenery and sewing costumes. It all seemed like a lot of fun, and none of it made her feel anxious.

"That would actually be really cool," Sandra concluded.

"Great!" Monica said.

Monica wasn't worried about Sandra. She wasn't a bad apple; she was just a kid who was lonely and disconnected and made a mistake because of her isolation. It was clear that all she needed was to connect. This was true of almost every student she had ever met; if they participated in extracurricular activities, they ended up much happier.

After they had set up a plan for Sandra to join the theater department, Monica found herself considering the strange paradox of our online lives. They promised a tool to connect all of us completely, and yet so often she saw the opposite result. *A screen is no substitute for real interaction,* Monica thought, *and the more we get these kids connected, the better they'll do.*

## Monica's Journal

### Adam Lustig on Student Conflict

- Bring the students in and meet with them in person.
  - Learn the root of the problem so you can help address that need.

### Tamara Givens on Social Media

- Students might not even really know what the actual conflict is about because the issue on social media has grown out of control.

- Social media is not the best for detailed communication. In-person communication is much better.
- Building relationships is the most important thing that an educator can do.
- School culture will go the way that campus relationships go.
- Activities are a great way to build relationships on campus.
  - They give students areas of support.

# CHAPTER TWENTY

# HEMISPHERES

"Frank," Cara said as she sat down next to Frank in the teacher's lounge, "I think it's time we settle this debate, once and for all."

Frank raised an eyebrow, wondering what Cara's point would be. Another boring series of logical inductions? A rant about how unreliable personal experience was? Already he was ready to defend himself and his personal politics. If he stuck to his guns, maybe even she would see, through his example, how important it was to listen to your gut, and hold on tight to your values.

"It's obvious," Cara continued, "that *Moving Pictures* was Rush's best album."

"No way!" Frank answered instantly, "Their best work is *Farewell to Kings*, hands down."

"How can you possibly be so absolutely wrong?" Cara joked. "Remember that, Frank? Arguing about fun things? I have to tell you, I'm tired of talking about politics."

"I agree!" Frank said. "It was better then, back when we would argue about best albums, or movies, or books. I mean, don't get me wrong; I appreciate being able to talk about political things with you too, but lately it just feels like . . ."

"Like it's all anyone talks about anymore? Like all of these failed actors and corrupt lawyers have stolen the spotlight for too long?" Cara ventured.

"Yes!" Frank said, "And I feel like we never solve anything. It's like this useless thing that's meant to pit us against each other, but then it never resolves. I'm just tired of it being everywhere and having everything be politicized."

"Exactly," Cara agreed, "so I was thinking . . . remember what you told me, years ago, about trying to stay solution-focused?"

Frank nodded.

Cara continued, "Well, our last conversation had me thinking. What can we do that would actually solve a political problem rather than just argue about it? And I realized there's one issue we both agree on adamantly . . ."

"I think I know where you're headed with this," Frank said, "getting the upper-level students in the school to vote."

"It wouldn't be too tough," Cara suggested. "We can set up a booth and show them how to get registered, and if we work together, we can create unbiased explanations of all the issues at hand."

"Sure, I'd be happy to do that," Frank offered, "but I think we should encourage them to find their own answers rather than offer ours, because I don't think I'd be able to keep my biases in check."

*I don't think you'd be able to, either,* Cara thought and almost said, but reminded herself of the point Monica had made: we're all on the same team. From that point of view, Cara recognized that Frank was offering an olive branch. She knew that he valued solidarity and comradery. Cara didn't care for self-degradation, but maybe that wasn't his goal; maybe he was trying to signal that he respected her, and this was his way of articulating that he'd hold his opinions if she would hold hers.

"Right," Cara agreed, "we should maintain neutrality."

Frank nodded in agreement. "That's a good way of putting it. We'll maintain neutrality."

Frank knew deep down that Cara wasn't the villain he had made her out to be in his mind throughout this election. He knew that he had been unfair. And now, as if to prove that point, here she was, suggesting that they teach students how to be more hands-on in life, which was what he had wanted most of all. Maybe she had been paying attention to what he'd been saying. Maybe she had been a team player all along, and he just hadn't seen it because he was too wrapped up in his own thoughts. Maybe it was time for him to start giving her the benefit of the doubt.

"This is a great idea," Frank said, and then added, "and *Moving Pictures* is a pretty good album."

"So is *Farewell to Kings*," Cara said.

# CHAPTER TWENTY-ONE

# REMEMBERING WHY

"Honestly, I'm just over it. I'm over all of it. I'm over all the sacrifice with nothing in return. I'm making less this year than I did last year, since they changed our health insurance premiums, and when I went to the doctor for that flu in the beginning of the year, I discovered that my copay is higher too. So I'm getting less across the board, and pay raises haven't kept up at all with inflation. Therefore, I'm receiving less now than last year. Why would I stay in an industry that doesn't take care of its people?" said Diane.

Diane leaned back in her chair, with a foot up on an extra chair kitty-corner to her and punctuated her explanation with a sip of her cortado. Monica listened carefully, actively empathizing with Diane's experience and imagining how it must feel.

"Meanwhile," Diane continued, "my sister left education and went corporate six months ago. You know how often she has to take her work back home with her at the end of the day? Never. For us it's just assumed that we'll be working when we get home to get done whatever is needed. And get this, they *approached her* to tell her that, due to inflation, they were issuing a company-wide raise. When I try to bring up anything like that, I'm met with someone in an office who doesn't have to deal with scrambling to manage an overpopulated classroom, telling me I'm just oh-so-very-appreciated but that right now, due to budget, blah blah blah. Rent goes up. Healthcare premiums go up. Heck, even the cost of my groceries goes up. The only thing that doesn't is what we're paid. And actually being a teacher? Man, it only gets worse and worse. I have no control over what I teach anymore, everything in the curriculum is geared toward taking standardized tests. There's nothing about critical thinking anymore. And some of these kids are smart enough to know that they're getting an "education" that doesn't actually have any real-world value. Honestly, it's . . . look, as I said, I'm over it. I appreciate you hearing me vent, but realistically, this is my last year. I'll finish out this semester and the next, and I'll do what they ask me to do, but after that, I'm out."

This wasn't the first time Monica had heard a teacher say these things. In fact, it had become a common theme. She had seen so many teachers get burned out for the reasons Diane had just outlined. Monica knew that they all came down to a simple truth: most teachers did not feel like they were being recognized or compensated fairly for the hard work that they were doing.

Monica, however, had come from the other side. She knew the corporate world. She understood that the grass always looks greener from the other side, but that it rarely ever is. In truth, "going corporate" had its own list of problems. There were pros and cons to both.

Monica considered where Diane was coming from. She considered how miserable it must have felt to feel overworked, underpaid, and unappreciated.

"Yeah," Monica agreed, "that's got to be frustrating."

"It is," Diane said, "and now here's the part where you say, 'but we're making a difference' or 'but the kids need us' or something like that, right?"

"No," Monica replied, trying hard to avoid feeling defensive, "I primarily planned on listening, but if you want to hear my point of view, I'm happy to share it with you."

"Sure," Diane said.

"You need to start telling admin 'no' when they ask you to do things," Monica said.

Diane raised an eyebrow.

"I'm serious," Monica said, "We all need to be better at setting boundaries. And if you're headed to the corporate world, you'd better cultivate that skill right now because I've been there, and I can tell you that you're definitely going to need it. Think of it this way, admin asks you to do something, and if you do it but you're unhappy doing it, do they really care? No, because they're just desperate to get it done. What are they going to do if you say 'no,' fire you? Unlikely. They're already struggling to hold on to teachers. I'm not saying to be mean about it. Say something like, 'Look, I can't do it because I'm already stretched too thin as it is. I care about the school, but I just can't do this, even though if I put myself in your shoes, I imagine I'd really need someone to jump on it. I want to help but I truly can't keep going like this,' Then what will they realize? That you're stretched thin enough to tell them 'no' and that you've taken on more than they probably even realized."

Monica continued, "Then figuring out who's going to take on the task becomes the admin's responsibility, not yours. More importantly, now they have to address you being stretched thin because they're going to realize that they're at risk of losing a highly experienced teacher."

"Okay," Diane sat up attentively, and set her coffee cup down, "that makes sense, but then what?"

"Then you need to work *with* them to find a solution. If you come at it from the point of view that you're adversaries, you won't get anywhere. If you come at it from a collaborative point of view, then you've at least got a shot," Monica explained.

"So what does that look like?" Diane asked.

Monica recognized that she had Diane's full attention. That was great news because it meant there was still at least a little part of her that wanted to teach.

"You give the benefit of the doubt, you assume they want the problem to be solved too, and that you're both on the same team. That enables you to be honest with them without making them feel defensive. That's the key. If you can do that, then you're collaborating rather than fighting."

"The thing I'm asking for, they can't give, that's the problem," Diane insisted.

"Yeah, maybe. You might be right, I honestly don't know for sure," Monica said, "but what if there are other options? If you let them know, 'Hey, I like this school, and I believe in it, but we've got to figure something out because I can't keep going this way,' then you've opened up a door where the two of you are working together toward a solution."

Diane considered the suggestion for a second, "And what if they can't do anything about it? What if they really can't help me in any significant way?"

"Then all you can do is accept that situation as it is, because that's reality, and make a choice based on that. I can see clearly that you've taken on more than most teachers, and the admin leans on you a lot. That's probably because you're their only option for most of these things. So, realistically, I see that you're doing what you can for the school, but if your needs aren't being met then you need to advocate for yourself by collaborating with them for a solution that works for you."

It was clear that Diane had not anticipated the school counselor coaching her on self-advocacy. She had expected instead that Monica would do some cognitive tap dance like she'd seen over and over again, hiding behind the students or using the term *hero* to try to exploit her good will.

In truth, that was what had upset Diane the most: the two-faced narrative that she had been fed over the past several years. On one hand, there was no money to spare, and more work to do, but on the other hand, everyone paraded around telling teachers that they were "heroes" and "on the front line" and a whole bunch of flowery words that didn't actually improve her situation at all. It was the way they rationalized the abuse.

But Monica was not offering any of that. She was being honest and straightforward. She was telling the truth, and that could only mean one thing.

"You care more about people than you do about your job," Diane realized.

"Yes," Monica said, "that's why I work in education. That's why I left my own cushy corporate gig a decade ago. And that's why I'm still here. A title is just a word. People are important."

Diane sat back, amazed. She could hardly believe it. Where had this been over the past three years? Was it absent from the people around her, or had she simply failed to recognize it? She had been, she realized, absolutely caught up in her own circumstances, and hadn't really been interested in the people around her. It was a horrible shock to realize she had been stuck in a negative funk, which had acted like a thick fog, concealing the human nature of the people around her. She was all at once reminded that her students were little people. Little people trying their best in a world that was so difficult to navigate. Her co-workers—when was the last time she had spent time with them outside of school? When was the last time she had really spent time with other human beings just for fun? What had happened? She felt as if she had been asleep for years and had just in this moment woken up to the existence of the human reality surrounding her.

Of course her pay was crap, and of course she was tired, but when had she ever thought money was the end-all-be-all of her life? She looked at the sneakers she had on her feet. They had all sorts of designs on them, drawn on in Sharpie by her students. There were little drawings of flowers and hearts, and a weird little character with big, goofy glasses and a circular nose and an ice cream cone in its hand that the class clown had drawn. It had a little speech bubble coming out of its mouth that read, "I love Mrs. Flynn more than ice cream!"

Diane realized that tears were beginning to well up in her eyes. She examined the quirky little illustrations scattered along her shoes. She recalled how the tradition had started, at the end of each year, when she retired her old shoes and had the exiting class design her new shoes. She remembered all those classes, year after year. She remembered how it felt to see her students realize something new for the first time. She remembered the gratitude that they expressed, in their own unique and bizarre way. She missed her kids. She missed them all so badly. They had all come and gone so quickly. In her mind's eye, she saw the overwhelming crowd of students she had known, all of them with their own unique perspective, all of them trying so hard to learn how to live. She saw the impact, the *true* impact, that teaching could have. Yes, the lip service really was just a tactic to keep teachers in the building, but that didn't matter.

The truth was that what she and her fellow teachers were doing was *even more* impactful than what they were told. They weren't heroes. That was a stupid word that assigned a ridiculous caricature to them that was like some guiding avatar for which they ought to strive. Heroes. Front-line workers. What nonsense. It wasn't that way. It was better than that. It was so much better than that, and none of the mass-manufactured catchphrases and buzzwords could ever hope to capture it, because they came from people who had never experienced the classroom themselves. Those sad souls had never taught a left-handed child how to write without smudging ink. Those miserable marketers had never witnessed the light that shined in a young person's eyes when they had finally grasped the true meaning of a new word. Those corporate, cubicle-chained cogs would never have shoes as valuable as these second-hand sneakers, no matter how much money they managed to squirrel away.

Diane had something more valuable than money. Diane had meaning.

Of course, Monica knew nothing of that inner monologue. From her point of view, all she saw was Diane staring at her shoes while her eyes started to water. Maybe it had been from the chill in the air. After all, fall was getting colder, and the wind was starting to carry the crisp edge that sometimes caused a person to tear up as it arrived.

Monica watched as the teacher finished her cortado, wiped her eyes and said, "Thanks, Monica. I think I was just in a funk. I probably won't quit, either. I think I was just feeling bummed, that's all."

Diane changed the subject then. And the two of them spent the remainder of their time together talking about the wild and crazy Halloween parties they had been to when they were younger.

# CHAPTER TWENTY-TWO

# DEFUSED

Harvey was not the imposing force that Mr. Dale had expected. For some reason, online, he seemed like he would be a fierce opponent. In person, he was not imposing at all.

He was lean, with large glasses and a thin mustache. He wore a short-sleeved button-up shirt, a pair of khaki shorts, and socks pulled high up onto his ankles.

His voice wasn't particularly loud, and he seemed to be almost timid in his approach to the conversation, as if the face-to-face encounter carried with it an intensity to which he was not accustomed.

Dale remembered Monica's advice: greet him warmly, and be sincere about connecting and collaborating. Assume good intent, and give him the benefit of the doubt. "Above all else," Monica had added, "don't hold any of the earlier conversations against him. Give the relationship a chance at a fresh start."

"I'm glad to meet you in person," Dale smiled warmly and put his hand out to Harvey, "and I really appreciate you helping us out."

"Nice to meet you too," Harvey shook Dale's hand, "and of course. Thank you for, uh . . . listening."

Dale had the option to interpret the "uh . . ." in a few ways. If he assumed the same mannerisms as the persona he had met online, it could clearly be interpreted as a passive aggressive insinuation that Dale wasn't actually listening. Alternatively, if Dale were to give him the benefit of the doubt and take this as a beginning, it could also have been a slightly uncertain hesitation from someone who was a little bit nervous.

Dale decided to give Harvey the benefit of the doubt.

"You're welcome," he answered.

The two of them sat down across from each other. They had decided to meet in Dale's classroom, which made it easier for Dale to have the information at hand and easy to present. It also offered him the opportunity to be welcoming and hospitable.

"Oh, hey, I keep a minifridge in here by the way, would you like a water or a soda or something?" Dale offered.

"Oh, sure. Thank you, that would, yeah, that would be nice actually."

As Harvey cracked open a root beer can, Dale set out to explain the situation.

"Okay," Dale said, "so here's where we need your help. You're absolutely right that this organization takes about 30% of what we raise, which is usually about $50,000 a year. So we might be missing out on almost 15 grand. Now a good chunk–roughly a third–of that goes to the prizes that the kids win, and I think that's okay, but I want to get your insight on that part too. Do you think that part of the system is okay?"

"Yeah, kind of," Harvey agreed, "the prizes are a little rinky-dink, but the kids are the ones doing the work so yeah, they should get rewards. I don't really know what else they could easily win."

"Good, okay. I think you're right," Dale said, "so we're looking at a value of about $40,000 to the school if we include the kids. Now here's where I need your help: if we can figure out a way to get $40,000 or more for the school without using this organization, then that would be ideal, because then we wouldn't even have to involve these guys at all. So let's brain-storm and come up with an alternative."

The two of them talked about the logistics of the fundraiser, and it soon became apparent that the organization offered more than just prizes. Harvey learned that not only did the organization run the final event, but their team consisted of four employees who were on campus for the three weeks prior, teaching leadership lessons, enhancing school spirit, and hyping the students up to raise money for their school. They also had an impressive marketing plan that the school simply couldn't come close to imitating through their own resources.

"Yeah . . ." Harvey finally concluded, "I guess right now I can't think of anything that could raise that kind of money."

"Yeah, me neither. But I think we should still keep an eye out," Dale agreed, "and if you come up with something then please reach out to me, because I do think that if we find a better option, we might go with it."

"For sure," Harvey said. "Honestly, I think if I knew this stuff, I probably wouldn't have been so combative. I just . . . well, you see there's always a lot of people trying to move money around. I see it all the time on the golf course, and sometimes it's not ideal. I just didn't want the school to get hosed like I've seen some people get hosed."

"Yeah, I definitely see where you're coming from," Dale agreed. "I'm not a businessperson, so I'm really glad to have a point of view from someone with more experience than me in this sort of thing. I've been doing fundraisers like these since I was in middle school, so I never really second-guessed them, you know? Anyway, I'm really glad we're on the same page, and I'm glad to have a critical thinker like you looking out for our school."

Dale suddenly realized a key part of what Harvey had said. He had almost missed it but had been listening just carefully enough to notice the real problem: a lack of information.

"Hey, Harvey," Dale added, "I think you're onto something. If I presented all this information to the parents online, in a video format or something similar, do you think it would be helpful?"

Harvey considered it for a moment, "Yeah, I think so. I think our biggest priority as parents is to be in the loop. Transparency would go a long way. Maybe we could have a live question and answer session so that all the parents could have a better understanding?"

"Great idea," Dale said.

The two of them exchanged goodbyes, and agreed that the fundraiser should continue on, at least for now. Harvey seemed much more at ease and even thanked Dale for speaking with him.

This man, Dale realized, wasn't an antagonist at all. He was just a father who wanted what was best for his kid and the school, and he had a way of going about that which was different from Dale's way. That didn't mean it was bad. They were all on the same team, united under the banner of Serenity Springs High School, and joined together in the hope that they could make life a little better for the next generation.

Dale felt better about everything. Only as the stress of the looming conflict came off of his shoulders did he realize how heavy it had been. It had caused him significantly more stress than he had even realized, and now it was over. The process had been a little painful. It was tough to put his ego aside after the heated conversations he'd had online, but the sting was nothing compared to the relief of having all of it behind him.

Harvey still wasn't the sort of person that Dale would choose to hang out with, but at the very least he helped him to realize that this was really a marketing issue and probably not much more. Ultimately, he was glad to have him as a team- mate rather than an enemy.

## Monica's Journal

### Dr. Mary Jane Hetrick on Communication

- First and foremost, make sure the complexity of the situation is communicated.
  - School situations are rarely binary. Sometimes there are laws, policies, or deeper reasons for implementing ideas in a school district.
  - School leaders should do a better job getting out in front of situations and communicate that extra layer of depth for their audience to better understand situations or decisions.
  - Communicate the why and the what, not just the facts.

### Emil Harker on Navigating Conflict

- First, we must assume good intent. This parent is sharing because they care.

- Second, we define and accept the reality of what is going on.
- Third, we figure out what we can do to help with the situation.
  - What does this parent need to feel good about this outcome?
  - How can we help them feel involved and valued?

## Tamara Givens on Marketing

- Make sure you work to market your programs and information to your parents/school community.
  - Posters are not marketing; they are publicity!
  - Marketing is intentional message placement in a variety of places and platforms.
  - Explain your why to your audience. Tell your story—before they do!

# CHAPTER TWENTY-THREE

# HARVEST

As the final bell rang on the last day before winter break, Monica felt herself exhale with relief. She had done it. Every single box on her checklist for the semester had been checked, and every conflict she had detected had been confronted. There was still work to do. There was always work to do, but things were looking up.

The students were cheerfully chatting up and down the halls, and Monica smiled as she passed by Diane who pointed out, "Look, Monica! Magic! Not a cell phone in sight!"

It was true. The kids had started to take to the idea that had been set in front of them that school was a place to put their phones away and be part of the community. The students were more connected than they had been before, and the peer-to-peer programs that Monica had begun were clearly beginning to yield results, especially among the younger students, who were striving to fit into the school's culture.

Student absences had begun to decline, and that was almost perfectly correlated with the recent increase in extracurricular participation. As Monica passed by the library, she saw that Dale's chess club was meeting with two students more than last week. He gave her a thumbs-up as she passed.

Cara and Frank sat behind their booth, encouraging the older students to register to vote, and helping them to understand each of the political issues one at a time.

Monica realized that the winter break had officially begun, but half the students remained in the school, participating in various community endeavors. She smiled. This was a community. This was her community.

She drove home, listening to a classic-rock radio station.

"Holy smokes. Since when is Nirvana *classic* rock?" Monica asked herself out loud as she drove.

She pulled up to her home, parked, and carried her bags inside. Then she put her laptop away, resolving not to touch it during her whole break. Monica knew that these breaks existed for a reason, and that time off was meant for enjoyment, reflection, and relaxation.

She walked over to her couch, kicked off her shoes, collapsed on it, and took a well-deserved nap.

When she awoke, she could hear Mike in the kitchen, preparing dinner. There was a little card on the coffee table in front of her. It read:

*For the best counselor ever.*

Monica smiled and reached out for the envelope, opening it up to see what was inside. She gasped when she saw its contents: inside were a pair of football tickets.

"Oh my goodness!" she called to Mike from the couch. "Thank you! We haven't been to a game in how long?"

"Two years," Mike said, "and all the rest is good to go, too. I think we *both* deserve a little time away, don't you?"

Monica shuffled, still waking up, into the kitchen. Waiting for her there was a nice hot plate of mac and cheese and a bowl of harvest fall salad.

"You're really racking up the points," Monica observed.

"I sure am! I'm on fire," Mike agreed, embellishing the statement with a little dance.

The two of them sat down to eat together, happy to have one another's company. There would be struggles later, undoubtedly; there would be conflicts and hardships and challenges that would seem, upon their arrival, to be formidable titans, but Monica knew right then, so strongly in that moment, that those conflicts were not the monsters they appeared to be. Each and every conflict, she understood, was an opportunity to improve this world just a little bit, and in the end that was all anyone could ever hope for.

# GOING DEEPER:
# Monica's Journal

Monica reviewed the notes she had amassed over the fall semester. She had taken out all of the most valuable lessons from her most influential mentors. She carefully examined the lessons from each one of them as she prepared for the second nine-week stretch of the school year. There was still work to be done, and these insights would prove valuable as she continued her work at Serenity Springs High School.

Review her journal entries below and watch the full expert interviews with author JC Pohl at teentruth.net/rising-above-interviews.

# Emil Harker, LMFT

Emil is an expert on conflict. He has been doing therapy for over 20 years. His passion is about getting through the fluffy stuff to the real nuts and bolts that help people deal with inevitable conflict with confidence. He has been on KUTV Channel 2's *Fresh Living* program for over 10 years. He is a frequent expert guest on several podcasts, radio, and TV programs. He has been a wilderness therapist, residential treatment center (RTC) therapist, parent trainer, and marriage therapist. His clients include professional athletes in the NBA, UFC, and NFL. He has his own podcast called *The Emil Show.* His book *You Can Turn Conflict into Closeness* has been well received by professional therapists and couples alike. His new book *Confidence in Conflict* is used in *Fortune* 500 companies helping them turn breakdowns into breakthroughs in business. Find out more about Emil at EmilHarker.com.

## Working Through Conflict in a Positive Way

- We need to rewire our ideas of conflict and respond in a different way.
  - This is resolved by hijacking the impulsive desire to become defensive.

- We can do this in four easy steps:
  - Sharing our feelings and reasons in a vulnerable way.
  - Using a transition statement such as "but if I see it from your point of view" or "if I look at it from your angle."
  - Then stating what you think it is like to be in the other person's shoes.
  - And lastly, checking in to see if you are right in stating how the person feels.
  - If someone is criticizing you, you need to learn the art of agreeing with what is true in their statement.
    - This takes the wind out of their sails.

## When School Leaders Feel Overwhelmed

- It is important to define and accept your reality.
- Come to a point where you can accept this new reality.
- Use this new reality to change your perspective about your job or your idea of success.

- The new paradigm shift will create motivation and energy!

## Engaging with Upset Parents or Parent Drama on Social Media

- First, we must assume good intent. This parent is sharing because they care.
- Second, we define and accept the reality of what is going on.
- Third, we figure out what we can do to help with the issue.
  - What does this parent need to feel good about this outcome?
  - How can we help them feel involved and valued?

## Helping Teachers Dealing with a Difficult Student

- Establish clear boundaries of what is expected in the class.

- Assume good intent in the reason the student is acting the way they are.
- Connect with the student before you correct.
- Let the student know that if they don't respect boundaries that something might have to change, and they will have to face consequences for their choices.
  - But the likelihood of this should be low if there is a connection built into the relationship.

## Supporting Teachers Who Might Be Burnt Out or Disengaged

- People will respond well when they feel like they are being a hero.
- But they won't respond well if they are not being treated like the hero they are.
- We need to pull them into the process to find the best solutions.
  - Connect and collaborate!

## Dealing with Students Engaged in Drama on Social Media

- We must equip students with the tools to deal with conflict.
- As earlier, this is resolved by hijacking the impulsive desire to become defensive.
  - We can do this in four easy steps:
    - Sharing our feelings and reasons in a vulnerable way.
    - Using a transition statement like "but if I see it from your point of view" or "if I look at it from your angle."
    - Then stating what you think it is like to be in the other person's shoes.
    - And lastly checking in to see if you are right in stating how the person feels.
- Teach students how to take the fuel away from the conflict.

## *Most Important Takeaway When It Comes to Positive School Conflict Resolution*

- *The relationship is the solution!*
- *As a school leader you are in a unique position to influence the lives of students, which in turn impacts our overall community.*
- *We want to build a society where people can work through differences in a collaborative way!*
- *Teaching conflict resolution in schools today will help with issues down the road.*

## Pete Getz, PhD

Dr. Pete Getz has a doctoral degree in Educational Administration with an emphasis on teacher leadership and program development. With over 25 years of experience working in public education, Dr. Getz has extensive familiarity with the comprehensive school setting and unique alternative education background. Dr. Getz specializes in student and staff wellness through research-based practices and an equitable, administrative school approach. He is currently serving as the principal of Valencia High School in Valencia, California.

### Working Through Conflict in a Positive Way

- Conflict is always happening on a campus, so we need to develop relationships in order to support people on our campuses.
- Remember that whatever the conflict is, it is important to them!
  - Work to connect with them in a relationship of empathy and compassion.
  - People in conflict need to feel heard.
    - The school leader is the person who can help that person feel heard.
- Empower staff members on campus to handle conflict before it gets to a school leader's office.
  - Everyone has a responsibility to the school community.
- Conflict has value; it can make people better.
  - You can learn something from every conflict you become engaged in.
  - It allows you to build up muscles and skills that you can use later.

- School leaders can actually see repetitive conflicts year over year, so gaining experience now can help with issues down the road.

## When School Leaders Feel Overwhelmed

- Connect to the elements of education that got you to where you are.
  - You are finally in the place where you wanted to be.
- School leaders should work to get other school leaders actively engaged in the school culture.
  - In the classrooms, the sports events, and the activities, model what involvement looks like!
- Practice self-care and a healthy balance between work and personal life.
  - Find things in your life that you enjoy and go do them!

## Engaging with Upset Parents or Parent Drama on Social Media

- As school leaders, we need to know that, no matter what we do, we can't please everyone.
- Be as transparent as possible.
- Strategize before an event or decision to punch holes in it and then get out in front of those issues.
- Be available for Q&A.
- Work to think your way through the marketing and PR angles of what you are doing on campus.
- Sometimes school leaders simply have to be able to develop a thicker skin.
  - Have boundaries established about who is actually involved in your community.
  - Don't put things in writing; pick up the phone. Invite them in. Hear them. And explain why.
    - Putting something in writing is like throwing gas on the fire.
  - Sometimes you can agree to disagree.

- And sometimes, on social media, no response is necessary.
  - If it is not a parent or student at your school, you probably don't need to address it.

## Helping Teachers Dealing with a Difficult Student

- This is simple: It is all about relationships.
  - We need to build environments where students feel safe and connected.
  - Get to know the students.
    - What is going on in their life that is causing the negative responses?
- We also must make it clear to the teacher that we support them, but we need them to build a relationship with the student to help solve the issue so we can find success in the classroom.
- Work to identify other activities or connections that you can build for the students on campus.
  - When kids are connected to schools, they have better grades and they show up more!

- Teachers sometimes have so much going on in their lives, but their classrooms are places where they have control.
  - It can be hard on them when they don't have that control with a student.
  - The relationship can help overcome these types of issues and helps teachers be more flexible in how they are getting their job done.

## Supporting Teachers Who Might Be Burnt Out or Disengaged

- A good school leader needs to know that changes on campus will negatively impact some staff members.
  - Be able to recognize this struggle and give them support during it.
  - If a teacher is struggling, we need to realize it is a big deal for that person.

## Dealing with Students Engaged in Drama on Social Media

- If you set a good climate and culture with great relationships, you can better handle these issues.
- Create a structure and avenue for these issues to be reported and dealt with.
- Come up with new and creative ways to handle these issues because traditional discipline options might not apply.
- Consider hosting social media education events and/or specific curriculum to teach students and parents about the issue.
- There can be opportunity here: You can use social media to help identify social-emotional wellness needs of students.

## Most Important Takeaway When It Comes to Positive School Conflict Resolution

- Find the one page of this book that jumps out and sticks with you!

> • Find the one idea or resource from this book that you can integrate on campus, and it will make the book worth it!

## Stephanie Eberts, PhD

Stephanie Eberts, PhD, LPC, is currently an assistant professor of professional practice at Louisiana State University and the coordinator of the school counseling track of the counselor education program. She has been training students to work as both school and clinical mental health counselors since 2010. Prior to working in higher education, Dr. Eberts worked as a school counselor in New Orleans as well as a counselor educator at Texas State University. Dr. Eberts is committed to her current students and the PK–12 students with whom they work.

> ### Working Through Conflict in a Positive Way
>
> • The more focus we put on relationships, the better the outcome can be.

- Leaders are being challenged right now, and that can heighten anxiety, thereby creating a spiraling attack on one another.
  - By having open and vulnerable conversations, leaders can help build relationships and solve conflict.

## When School Leaders Feel Overwhelmed

- A lot of our educators and educational leaders are feeling burnt out.
  - The solution is for them to continue to educate because that is what they are good at.
  - They have to take it upon themselves to educate the community.
    - Help other people to understand what teachers do on a day-to-day basis.
    - Discuss how parents can participate, and how people can become part of the school culture.
- We're losing educators because they're burning out.

- Instead of a top-down model, we could use a collective, collaborative model. That way it's not just a superintendent saying, "Hey, you need to do this."
  - The feeling that's received by teachers is "you've been doing it wrong," even though that's not what's being said.
- We need to get parents involved in an appropriate way, making a concerted effort in building those relationships so people can work together and collaborate on campus.
  - This creates ownership. We need the parents to feel like "this is ours, not just something that's happening over there."

## Engaging with Upset Parents or Parent Drama on Social Media

- Connect with the moderators of the social media group to encourage good moderation of the group when arguments flare up.

- Invite the leader of the parents who are upset in and have a personal conversation with them.
  - Seek to understand them, but also be prepared to educate them on all aspects of the issue and how it benefits the school/students.
  - Work with them to go back and educate other parents.
- School leaders need to make sure they are advocating for and marketing their school programs.
  - Education is our craft, so business and marketing skills might require additional training.

## When Staff Member Politics or Arguments Impact School Culture

- Mediation can help with these issues.
  - Find commonalities and compromise.
  - Help people to humanize each other. We are more than just our political opinions.

- It is not about trying to change someone's mind; it is about helping these people make a personal connection.
- There also can't be a punitive element to the mediation.
  - If teachers have this experience and it is positive, they can maintain that momentum for conflicts and issues with their students.
- When we build relationships, we create more security in our school community.
- Our job is to create a school culture where people feel safe, cared for, and connected. Positive results will follow!

## Helping Teachers Dealing with a Difficult Student

- Consider giving the student a leadership role on campus or something that they can be a part of.
  - In doing this, they will feel cared for and seen.

- Help the student find their tribe and connection on campus.
- Ask the teacher to find ways to build a true relationship with the difficult student.
  - Conversations with the student.
  - Positive labeling with regard to who the student is.
  - Giving the student some responsibility in the classroom.
- Spend time with your students to build up currency for when times are difficult.

## Supporting Teachers Who Might Be Burnt Out or Disengaged

- Look at school culture first and determine how this teacher is not connected to it.
- Try to figure out what the problem is in the system that is affecting that teacher.
- Work to see if this is something that can be worked on in collaboration.
- Showing this teacher respect can help revitalize them.

- Realize that sometimes, in some situations, teachers need a vacation, a break, or maybe even a transfer to a different school.

## Dealing with Students Engaged in Drama on Social Media

- Realize that adults have fully developed brains and students do not.
- Educate students and parents on the impacts of social media.
  - Use real-world stories of social media issues to educate kids about outcomes and consequences.
- Work to build a culture of safety and compassion at school that will spill over into social media.
- Work to bring face-to-face student mediation into this type of situation.
  - Form mediation contracts with the students.
- Encourage parents to manage their student's social media time/access.

_Most Important Takeaways When It Comes to_
_Positive School Conflict Resolution_

- _People need healing right now._
  - _Work to provide an environment where that healing can take place._
  - _School culture is the answer for everything and we set that by example!_

## Mary Jane Hetrick, PhD

Mary Jane Hetrick, PhD, has a doctorate in public policy and public administration from Auburn University. She taught graduate-level classes for over a decade, both in the classroom and online. Dr. Hetrick has dedicated immense time to public education, including serving on a local board of trustees, a statewide organization serving local school boards, and a local education foundation. She is currently sitting as the school board president for Dripping Springs Independent School District and serves as a board member for the Texas Association of School Boards.

# Working Through Conflict in a Positive Way

- Coming from a place of service can help you find your way in school leadership.
- Knowing who you are and what your core values are can help you stand strong in the face of conflict.
- As a school leader, you need to keep governance at the forefront of your efforts in order to maintain the overall direction of the organization.
  - One or two issues can't affect the larger work of the entire district or school.
- Religious faith can be a great way to maintain moral values in the face of conflict.
  - "There, but for the grace of God, go I."
  - It is important for school leaders to forgive and move forward.
- School boards in particular come from a place of governance, which can be very different from hands-on leadership.

- Remember that the superintendent is actually the person in charge of the district staff, students, and so forth.
- Working together will benefit students and staff more than working against each other.
- Know your district's short-term, midterm, and long-term plans and empower leadership to execute them.

## When School Leaders Feel Overwhelmed

- Try to have vision-oriented conversations before this happens.
  - What kinds of supports are in place?
  - Are these supports in place at all campuses? Are they the same?
  - Clear policy making is kind to staff, parents, and students.
- Make sure school leaders are supported with an administrative team.

- Layers of support around principals can help manage communication and strategies.
- Make sure good training is in place for new administrators coming up to assistant principal roles.
- We need coherence throughout the entire system.
- This raises morale and enhances relationships.

## Engaging with Upset Parents or Parent Drama on Social Media

- First and foremost, make sure the complexity of the situation is communicated.
  - School situations are rarely binary . . . Sometimes there are laws, policies or deeper reasons for implementing ideas in a school district
  - School leaders should do a better job getting out in front of situations and communicate that extra layer of depth for their audience to better understand situations or decisions.

- Communicate the why and the what, not just the facts.
- Don't be afraid to invite people in to have a face-to-face conversation.
  - This will fundamentally change the relationship. It makes each person human!
- We need to make sure we are educating the public about the deeper elements of these issues.

## When Staff Member Politics or Arguments Impact School Culture

- Create a trail of resolution, there should be a chain of command within the system to resolve issues like this.
  - It is the principal's job to set expectations and communicate culture for all staff members.
  - Are policies, procedures, and programs in place to handle this type of situation?
    - If not, create them!

### Helping Teachers Dealing with a Difficult Student

- Make sure that support staff is placed within the system to help the teacher.
  - Use counselors, mentors, and other staff members who can help.
  - This allows the teacher to focus on the aspects of teaching the child.
  - Personalized learning can be done well if we tap into the students' innate strengths.
    - Consider using the Strengths Finder Assessment

### Supporting Teachers Who Might Be Burnt Out or Disengaged

- Make sure professional development opportunities are available for staff.
  - This can help light their fire again.
- Consider cross-curricular collaboration and teaching techniques to give teachers more depth in their experience of teaching.

- This could create ways to build on the strengths of teachers as they work together.
  - Perhaps switch students between teachers if needed/desired.

## Dealing with Students Engaged in Drama on Social Media

- Create programs in which students come together in service for others.
- Bring in programs or curriculum to help students understand that what we see on social media is largely pretend or just the best of people's lives.
  - Assess whether students understand this.

## Most Important Takeaway When It Comes to Positive School Conflict Resolution

- Often, when people have polar opposite views, they can find middle ground if they simply meet together in person and discuss.

> • *Connect as humans first before seeking to understand the issues around the conflict.*

## Tamara Givens

Tamara Givens has been teaching high school since 1989, starting out as an English teacher and yearbook adviser. In 1996, she made the move to help open Granite Bay High School and in 1999 accepted the position of activities director, which she has held since then. She has been a district Teacher of the Year recipient and has been active in the California Association of Directors of Activities for over two decades, serving for 10 years on the Area A council.

> *Working Through Conflict in a Positive Way*
>
> • *The conflicts in our society create anxiety for educators and students.*
> • *Sometimes just doing your job can make people upset, but we have to push through in the best way we can.*

- When there is real conflict in our school community, we have to find ways to reach out and build bridges.
- We need to make sure that every single student has at least one key person that they can talk to.
- Activities are a great way to build relationships on campus.
- This gives students areas of support.

## When School Leaders Feel Overwhelmed

- We have to remember why we got into education in the first place.
  - Life is a journey, not a destination.
  - We can get through everything eventually.
  - Always remember what is best for kids.
- Focus on building relationships with staff above all.
  - This gives administrators a group of people that can support them and help them not feel alone.

○ The team is what can give you the personal energy to move forward.

## Engaging with Upset Parents or Parent Drama on Social Media

- Ignore issues on social media as best you can.
- If it is important, the parents can contact you directly.
- If you can't ignore it, you have to get people in a room to discuss the concern.
  ○ Not on social media. In person!
  ○ Get the most influential people together so you can build momentum.
  ○ Collaborate to find out-of-the-box solutions.
- If you can work to build relationships today, they may help you down the road when negative things happen.
- Make sure you work to market your programs and information to your parents/school community.
  ○ Posters are not marketing; they are publicity!

- Marketing is intentional message placement in a variety of places and platforms.
  - Explain your why to your audience. Tell your story—before they do!

## When Staff Member Politics or Arguments Impact School Culture

- Principals should be the people to handle these types of issues; they are the people in charge of the staff.
- School leadership needs to work to pull people together.

## Helping Teachers Dealing with a Difficult Student

- Engage parents in helping you work with the student.
- Sometimes it can be best to move the student to a different class.
  - Maybe they can find a different teacher on campus they can relate to in a better way.

- You can't be every kid's "person," but maybe someone else on campus can be.
- Be patient with students. Remember that they are maturing and growing over the time they are on your campus.
- Work to help students get connected on campus to a group of people who can support them.
- If you are going to meet with the student, get someone else in the room so you are not meeting alone. A third-party voice can help find middle ground.

## Supporting Teachers Who Might Be Burnt Out or Disengaged

- This can happen often. We don't want it to, but it does.
- Help the teacher find something else on campus that they can contribute to, what they care about doing on campus, and support them in that.

- *Find ways to show appreciation to teachers and staff members.*
- *Usually it is not the kids that cause this; it is the adults that burn the teachers out.*
  - *Work with teachers to foster friendly relationships on campus.*
  - *Help teachers find what they are passionate about on campus.*

## Dealing with Students Engaged in Drama on Social Media

- *Get your school resource officer (SRO) involved.*
  - *Bring the kids together and discuss the situation with the SRO.*
  - *Help students see the SRO as a caretaker and not a cop.*
- *Students might not even really know what the actual conflict is about, because the issue on social media has grown out of control.*

○ *Social media is not the best for detailed communication. In-person communication is much better.*

• *Offer a system for students to anonymously report issues on social media.*

## Most Important Takeaway When It Comes to Positive School Conflict Resolution

• *Building relationships is the most important thing that an educator can do.*

• *School culture will go the way that staff relationships go.*

## Adam Lustig

Adam Lustig is currently the director for leadership services and training at the National School Boards Association (NSBA) where he works to promote positive and safe learning environments for all students, while addressing historical inequities and providing training, support, and directives to help support all students throughout our nation's public schools. Adam has also worked in New York City and Washington, DC, public schools as a teacher, coach, school administrator, and central office manager overseeing school safety, climate and culture, social-emotional learning, restorative justice and bullying prevention. His work focuses on ensuring that schools actively build positive communities, fostering academic, behavioral, and social/emotional growth and resolution.

## Working Through Conflict in a Positive Way

- A simple solution is modeling the behaviors.
- How are we as school leaders conducting ourselves on campus, in meetings, and on social media?

## When School Leaders Feel Overwhelmed

- Separate yourself from the issues.
- People will make it personal, but your mindset has to stay on the issues.
- You can't do it alone. Who are your supports in the district and are communication lines open?
- Be able to listen and understand when attacks are coming at you, so you can understand the root causes, themes, and issues at play.

- Escalating conflict gets us going in a circle and not where we want to be headed.
- "You don't build the roof in the middle of the storm."
  - We need to build up our capacity and thoughts on our social-emotional skills before the storm happens.
  - If you want to drive culture, this has to be part of your being and what you are bringing to campus.

## Engaging with Upset Parents or Parent Drama on Social Media

- We don't need to always feel the need to respond, especially on social media.
- Examine the situation. What information was possibly not given out ahead of time?
- Connect directly in person with the parent or group.

- Use social media to communicate the story of your campus.
  - Do not to engage in arguments or put fuel on the fire on social media.

## When Staff Member Politics or Arguments Impact School Culture

- We need to have core values in our school community so that, when conflict becomes polarizing, we have basic core values we can all connect back to.
  - Our actions should be aligned with these core values.
- As an administrator, we need to have the pulse of the building: How are these arguments affecting everyone else?
  - Identify root causes and help to meet those needs.
  - Help to find common ground.

- Provide restorative conversation for staff members in conflict, and work to find out what each person needs to feel heard/valued in your community.
  - Work with each person (beforehand) individually to understand what happened, how they feel, and what do they need moving forward.

## Helping Teachers Dealing with a Difficult Student

- First and foremost, look to hire people who genuinely care about kids.
- Hire people who can emulate your core values.
- Offer training so teachers can be aware of issues students are bringing to campus.
- Offer training to de-escalate issues in the classroom.
- Recognize that not every student will connect with you. Know when to tap out and pull someone else in.

- Create a plan with your support team so you know what to do when issues arise.
- Consider hiring from certification programs that include additional information on social-emotional issues so that staff members are better informed in their approach to these issues.

## Supporting Teachers Who Might Be Burnt Out or Disengaged

- Make sure we are focusing on the social-emotional wellness of our staff.
  - What type of supports are we providing?
- Make sure we are bringing the disengaged persons to the table so they have representation and are involved.
- Recognize that teaching is a grind, so celebrate and recognize the work of teachers!
- Keep building community and relationships at the core of your work.

### Dealing with Students Engaged in Drama on Social Media

- Have clear protocols and practices on social media on and off campus.
- Understand when something is escalating and could impact the safety of your campus.
- Bring the students in and meet with them in person.
  - Learn the root of the problem so you can help address that need.

### Most Important Takeaway When It Comes to Positive School Conflict Resolution

- Make your school climate part of your philosophy, not just a program. It needs to be part of who you are!

# ABOUT THE AUTHORS

## JC Pohl

JC Pohl is an award-winning producer, nationally recognized speaker, and certified counselor who has reached more than 11 million people in 7,000+ schools. He has produced groundbreaking programs such as TEEN TRUTH and RISING UP, and award-winning content for companies like Warner Brothers, ESPN, and Disney. He has also provided innovative educational content for the American Film Institute and Human Relations Media.

His school culture work with TEEN TRUTH has sent him around the world, inspiring students, educators, and parents to tell hard truths and be the difference. During his career, Pohl has been featured on news programs, podcasts, and has received front-page coverage on *USA Today* as well as *Yahoo! Sports*. He has personally reached students in every type of school you can imagine and keynoted countless educational conferences across North America.

Pohl is a Licensed Marriage and Family Therapist (LMFT) in the state of Texas and is the author of *Building School Culture from the Inside Out* as well as *Building Resilient Students from the Inside Out* and *Building Campus Relationships from the Inside Out*. You can find him on Facebook and LinkedIn or connect directly at www.jcpohl.com.

## Ryan McKernan

Ryan McKernan is a writer based in Austin, Texas.

He can probably still do an ollie, teaches rock climbing at a local high school, and is remarkably average at chess. Follow him on Instagram at @thefinalryan.

More information at jcpohl.com or teentruth.net

# INDEX

in conflict resolution, 133
for difficult students, 146–149
in marriage, 4–5, 123
for school leaders, 15, 69, 71
for staff members, 33, 35,
   97–98, 104, 169–170
TEEN TRUTH (film
   series), xv, xvii
teentruth.net, 193
Texas Association of School
   Boards, 213
Texas State University, 206
Thick skin, on social
   media, 202
Top-down models, 208
Trail of resolution, 217
Transfers:
   for difficult students, 77–78,
      142, 146, 223
   for teachers, 45, 212
Transition statements, 85,
   139, 195, 198
Transparency, 48, 185, 202
Trust, 12, 142
Truth, 134, 135, 195

**U**

Upset parents:
   Stephanie Eberts
      on, 208–209

Pete Getz on, 202–203
Tamara Givens on,
   222–223
Emil Harker on, 196
Mary Jane Hetrick on,
   216–217
Adam Lustig on, 228–229
school leaders' conflicts
   with, 13–14, 70–72,
   132–135
"Us versus them" mentality,
   83–84, 99–100

**V**

Vacations, 45, 212
Valencia High School, 199
Violence, 83–84
Vision-oriented discussions, 215
Voter registration, 168–169, 190
Vulnerability, 70, 85, 134, 139, 195

**W**

Walking meetings, 97, 131, 137
Work life, balance of personal
   and, 16, 68, 201

**Y**

*You Can Turn Conflict
   into Closeness*
   (Harker), 80, 194